"I highly reco
delivers a ste~ ~,
strengths, intensifying them and using them ~~
path to personal, authentic success. It is a powerful and
empowering tool I will keep with me and refer back to again
and again." –

Ruth Wariner,
Speaker and Author of the New York Times Bestseller, *The*
Sound of Gravel

———————

"I highly recommend this book as it will change your view on
leadership, yourself and the world! If you are a looking to
stand out and move up, this is the right book for you. It will
also make you much more successful, in no time. Both Linda
McCabe and Sarah Victory are subject matter experts and
power contacts that you want to have in your network!!"

Kevin Piket,
Vice President of Sales & Marketing,
BlueStar Technology

———————

"Sarah and Linda have a remarkably practical yet effective
approach to helping business leaders achieve both "power"
and "success" in their professional lives. Their book not only
provides the tools and techniques needed to communicate
and market effectively, but also helps to instill a sense of
confidence and motivation – all of which are crucial to
ultimately achieving professional success. How to be
Powerful is a worthy read."

S. Jarret Raab,
Litigation Partner, Williams, Bax & Saltzman, P.C.H

"As an entrepreneur, you've got to be great at three things: leadership, getting and holding people's attention with your ability to speak, and sales. Own these skills, and your a powerful competitor, capable of leading the field. Miss any of the three, and you're an also-ran. Sarah and Linda show you the highway to power mastery. Grab this book, read it with pen in hand, do the exercises, and you'll gain skills your competition doesn't have. I have personally benefitted from the ideas in this book, using the techniques to build a seven-figure business and lead my customers to new levels of success."

Mark S A Smith,
Author and executive strategy coach working with
executives to sustainably grow their business.

"I am thrilled to own a copy of this book. I had the pleasure of personally working with both Linda McCabe and Sarah Victory as business coaches to help take my business to the next level. I was not sure how to take the company that I started from a one-man shop to a team of 14, but through working with Linda in formulating a strategy to grow the business over time and with Sarah to create internal systems, I surpassed my original goals and achieved more success within my own business. I cannot thank them enough for their guidance and their experience and am excited that they are now sharing the wealth!"

Anthony Navarro,
Owner, Liven It Up, Wedding & Event Consultant

"How to be Powerful is easily one of the most clearly practical and relevant skill development leadership books I've read. Linda McCabe and Sarah Victory shared this timely and important work. I highly recommend it from my heart!"

Valencia Ray, M.D. and author

"I'd recommend this book to anyone who has ever felt the desire to be an inspirational leader, wants more yesses from prospects, and needs confidence to speak from the stage, BUT deep-down they're being held back by fear, a sense of powerlessness, or flat-out immobilized. Grab a pen and paper because in this book, Linda and Sarah will coach you with practical exercises designed to interactively guide you into the action of finding your power to lead, to sell, and to speak."

Mark Repkin,
Sales Performance Coaching & Consulting Interim and VP of Sales for Growth Oriented SMB's

———

"Sarah Victory and Linda McCabe are engaging and powerful professionals who have the ability to immediately get to the heart of the matter and offer practical insights and guidance. Their book does the same: offers powerful concepts and immediately engages readers in exercises that can't help but leave them with valuable insights and ideas. The book is expertly crafted and leads readers through a transformative journey."

Amy Riley,
Shoop Consulting Group, Inc., Training & Development Consulting and Leadership Coach

———

"After reading the first paragraph in this book I was hooked. The way it is laid out, from the worksheets to the examples, I just couldn't wait to get to the next page. If you are looking for a book that will guide you to becoming a better sales person, leader, speaker, or just a better you, this is the book to read. I have read numerous books from Zig Ziglar, Brian Tracey ,and Tony Robins and I can say that this book is right up there with them and is in many ways better."

Sid Rothenberg,
President, Reliable Information Technology, Inc.

"How to be Powerful" by Sarah Victory and Linda McCabe is a must-read for all small business owners. Through their extensive experience, Sarah and Linda give us profound yet easy to understand concepts on how to be brilliant in our work. I especially love the "Container System" for time management because it provides a system to allocate your time in your business and personal life. I also love the "Magic Mirror" concept. What a great idea to take note of positive comments people say about us. There are so many awesome stories and exercises in this book. Sarah and Linda are inspirational storytellers, and they have written a book that will have a life-changing impact."

Maritess Bott, JD, MSA,
Bott & Associates, Ltd.

————————

"How to Be Powerful is a must have for the leader who wants to stand out and get noticed. The book is full of stories and real strategies you can implement right away, from mapping out how to grow your business to getting more speaking engagements. How to Be Powerful has changed my business for the better."

Tiffany S. Hinton,
Bestselling author and GF Mom Certified

————————

"Sarah Victory and Linda McCabe are extraordinary coaches and teachers. This book captures the essence of the work they have done with so many leaders to help them excel in their careers. The book leaps past leadership jargon and convincingly prescribes solutions to the blocks that holds so many people back from being successful. Read this book, you will be glad you did!

Sabrina Braham, M.A. PCC,
Executive Coach and Founder of
WomensLeadershipSuccess.com. radio podcast.

"In their new book, How to be Powerful, Sarah Victory and Linda McCabe share secrets gained from their personal lives and their distinguished professional careers working with hundreds of clients. Their theme of how to project personal power is stressed throughout all three sections of the book— in leadership, sales, and speaking. The book is filled with exercises, examples, and techniques drawn from the authors' own experiences and those of their clients, and I highly recommend it for anyone who would like to feel more confident personally, more comfortable in sales conversations, or more capable as a public speaker."

Elaine Quinn,
The Solopreneur Specialist® Chicago

———————

"I am thrilled to see Sarah Victory and Linda McCabe teamed up for a book about being powerful. Both Sarah and Linda are amazing business leaders who I have learned from time and time again in my years of being a small business owner. Linda brings tactful skills and organization to small business and Sarah brings voice and speech to business leaders. Their book, How to be Powerful, shares amazing tips for being confident, effective and influential. It is a great read for current and striving leaders alike."

Alexandra Eidenberg,
Small Business Owner, Community Activist, Mom

———————

"Individually these women are nothing short of inspirational, but together, this dynamic duo pack a punch. The "AHA" moments received are beyond motivating. They provide step by step tools that not only tweak and guide your thought process but also push you into creating an actionable strategy that will take your business to the next level."

Carmen Londoño,
Managing Partner, The Insurance People

"This book is a quick read filed with compelling information and valuable exercises, jam packed with great foundational tools for any business owner and organizational leader. Over the years, I've made multiple referrals for Sarah and Linda, without fail they have received rave reviews and hired on many occasions; this book is a testament to why they have enjoyed such success and how they have helped others recognize similar triumphs in their endeavors."

Eric Lazar,
SpeedPro Chicago Loop, Partner & Lead Evangelist

————————

"Victory and McCabe have taken a pragmatic and realistic view of human behavior as it relates to the power that leadership entails in this era. No man is an island and it has never been truer than in this era of instant communications. They make sense of it all by enlightening the reader with readily implementable tools and philosophies to help leaders to be powerful but not boorish, confident but not cocky and infinitely less fallible by strategizing, communicating and executing for stability and sustainability. This is a critical read for those that need and want to harness the human spirit to make gains for more than just themselves."

Fred Stephenson,
Vice President, North Coast Capital Advisors Ltd.

How to be Powerful

Insider Secrets to Brilliant Leadership, Sales, and Speaking

Sarah Victory and Linda McCabe

We want to dedicate this book to our wonderful husbands and family, and to the terrific clients we have had the honor to have worked with along the way.

Foreword

To be powerful, it seems to me, you need to do three things:

1) Make the decision to be powerful

2) Conduct yourself and relate to others from a position of compassionate strength, and

3) Communicate to those you work with and those outside your workplace in a way that is clear, memorable, and meaningful.

I bet I know what you're thinking:

"Heh. That's easy for you to say. But when I actually try to do those things, a million speed bumps get in the way."

OK. Whether or not that's what you were thinking, that is in fact what happens to most people. And then what follows is usually tragically disappointing, either way:

- You lose confidence, and give up trying, or

- You decide this wholistic, emotionally aware method of leadership is a bunch of academic hogwash, so you're just going to go about it the old way. And you resign yourself to let the chips fall where they may.

Um, excuse me. Hopefully not you.

Because now, finally, two women who have blazed trails at the top levels of their respective professions with their own work have taken the long, lonely, but ultimately redeeming and fulfilling road of writing this book. So you can get to a third option, which, rather than being disappointing, is satisfying and deeply meaningful.

By that I mean: Becoming a powerful and persuasive leader, while retaining full ownership of your soul. Coming across to others (and, most importantly, yourself) like a full-fledged human being. Actually liking what you're doing – a lot – and being surrounded by others who feel the same way about you (most of the time, anyway).

Now this would be a pipe dream except for two things:

First, Sarah Victory has been through tragedies and challenges most people couldn't even imagine. She has remained a kind and extraordinarily competent person. As a speaker and persuader, Sarah is one of the most talented people I've ever met.

And she has helped hundreds of people expand their vision of success and start to live it fully. I've known Sarah for more than 20 years and I've also experienced some major breakthroughs myself as a result of her brilliance.

Second, Linda McCabe has succeeded in one of the most rough-and-tumble businesses known to man or woman: scrap metal. She took a failing company and turned it around so the financial statements were mighty impressive.

Through it all, she still kept her warm and caring side alive and thriving. In her "second life" as a coach, she has helped hundreds of others blaze their own trails and attain a personal version of success that makes their lives better. Her love of life and generosity shine brightly in the pages you are about to read.

If you are younger than I am (I've been in business more than four decades), I envy you. I've always had questions about power and leadership. Something I saw years ago didn't sit right with me. I didn't know what it was, but I sensed something was wrong, in a widespread way.

Worst of all, I didn't know what to do instead.

I've learned a lot over the years, and what's in this book consolidates what I've already learned and, importantly, expands upon it. So, again, if you are younger than I, then I envy you because I wish I had had access to this book when I was your age.

If you are a Senior Boomer such as myself (laughing as I write this), then, welcome to the future of power and leadership. Hey, we can't screw things up much more than we already did, right? But we can do much, much better – and I think you'll be pleasantly surprised, as I was, to see how Sarah and Linda are doing a very practical job of leading the way.

David Garfinkel
Author and Business Coach
San Francisco

Table of Contents

Introduction

After coaching over 700 clients between the two of us and speaking to over 1000 audiences, the thing that became most clear was that what people really want is to be powerful in their Leadership, Sales, and Speaking abilities.

Linda recalls a client who felt confused and overwhelmed about what kind of work he was doing and what he really wanted to do. He couldn't even begin to identify what kind of business he wanted to have. He questioned whether he even had what it would take to be successful. Fast forward three years and he has a thriving, successful business, has numerous employees, is one of the most powerful businesses in his industry in the U.S. and has won multiple awards.

Sarah was doing a seminar when she looked out at the audience and said, "If I could do magic and sprinkle fairy dust over your head, and you could have anything you want, feel as powerful as you like, what would you want?"

One young woman meekly put up her hand and said, "I would have a New York Times bestselling book, I'd be on Oprah, and speak around the world to millions of people."

People in the audience giggled but Sarah saw something in this woman and took her aside after the seminar. She asked if the woman would like to work with her and she said yes. Two years later the young woman had a New York Times bestselling book, was on Oprah, and has since spoken to millions of people around the world.

These are just two of the many experiences that Linda and Sarah have had and it's what drives them to help more people find their power and succeed.

According to Merriam-Webster.com the definition of powerful is *having the ability to control or influence people or things*. Our definition is similar and for our clients it is the ability to make things happen. It is having the "how-to's" to create results in order to get what they want. It is having the freedom, both financial and personal, to make life easier and better. And, above all, it is having the ability to serve others.

Often we have heard people express concern about being powerful with the false assumption that to be powerful is to have power *over* others rather than *with* others. All of us as human beings enrich the world by having power *with* others. Those people who have chosen to have power *over* others are the tyrants of the world and they are not truly powerful. They will never experience the joy of sharing their gifts to the betterment of the world. So this distinction is important for our readers to understand. We hope you will strive for truly being powerful and that you will share your talents with others.

"Our deepest fear is not that we are inadequate. Our deepest fear is that we are powerful beyond measure"

Marianne Williamson

We have found that a common thread among many of our coaching clients is a fear of success. This is related to being powerful. The fear might be that if you are successful and become powerful you might lose more than you gain. For example, many clients say to us "I want to be successful, but not at the expense of my family."

Or, "I want to be successful, but not at the expense of my health." So power and success don't necessarily mean giving up other things.

On the other hand, many people feel that they are not worthy of power and success. In fact, some of our clients tended to set up blocking mechanisms so they wouldn't reach the level of success they could potentially reach.

You deserve to be powerful and successful.

Below, write down five reasons why you want to be powerful. When you do this, let your ideas flow and do your best to avoid editing. Examples might be, "I want to be more powerful because I will grow as a person, I can help others, or I will have the means to do more in my life, etc." Your answers might also be as simple as "I want a new car or home."

1. _____
2. _____
3. _____
4. _____
5. _____

As coaches for many years, we've noticed that some people run with all the ideas we give them and others take more time to absorb and apply our suggestions. Be patient with yourself as you grow in your power and evolve as a human being.

We promise you when you do the things we suggest in this book, you will become more powerful! Although you may have to alter your behavior in some way, it doesn't necessarily mean that you will lose anything. In fact, you will gain beyond your wildest imagination.

Section One
Leadership

Chapter One

Finding your Confidence

In order for us to be the best leaders, we must be sure of ourselves. If others are to follow, we must be strong and trust ourselves. Any action cannot take place without power. For us to help others, we must accept that we have to be powerful. That power, in part, comes from valuing what we offer. If we doubt what we have to give, we diminish our capacity to lead well.

Once we have the awareness of our value, we must have the confidence to move forward and succeed. Having power and confidence is essential. However, we must add systems and processes to complete the picture.

There exists in each of us an unfortunate habit of playing up our shortcomings. The balance is off and we see the negatives too often instead of the positive aspects of who we are and what we can become. Have you ever wished for a genie or a magic guru who could transform you into your very best self? In this chapter, we're going to reveal the secret to help you do just that.

Now, meet the magic mirror. This concept came about with our experience of working with hundreds of our coaching clients. We have noticed that our clients tend toward a propensity to overlook their own brilliance.

Imagine holding a mirror to yourself and seeing only those parts which are the rich expressions of your talent, skills, and value that you bring to the world. It's not always easy to do this because one is so practiced in self-judgment. Actually, that is a habit that self-perpetuates. And, people learn this early and continue it into adulthood.

A big part of the reason people come to us is that we see their genius and we can show them how to exploit that genius. First, you have to be aware of it. We had one client who came to us who was doing a fabulous job. Business was booming. She was growing her business at a rate of 25% a year. Her employees loved her and yet she couldn't see all that she was doing right. She seemed only to focus on the miniscule negatives. When we began to reveal her true value to her, she began to blossom.

Exercise

Write down all the qualities about yourself that you would see in the Magic Mirror. Remember, if a thought pops up that doesn't capture your greatness, set it aside, and keep writing about what is positive about you. It helps to recall a time when someone made you feel loved or was a staunch supporter who reflected how wonderful you really are.

_____

_____

_____

_____

_____

What did some of the staunch supporters and loved ones say that you can add to your list? The Magic Mirror serves as your guiding light for whenever you need to find your power. When you see that power in yourself, you are better equipped to see it in others. Use that power to help those you lead.

One challenging aspect to maintaining good leadership is developing strategies that help you to hold on to your power. As in all things, there is an ebb and flow with our feelings of power.

Depending on your life circumstances at any given time, you may diminish your power. In order to sustain the confidence which enhanced your power, you need the source of it, which was our Magic Mirror. Keep your list in a place where you can either see it or readily find it. In fact, mark your calendar to review it once each month.

Also, decide to stay vigilant about capturing comments that people make about you that are positive. People have a tendency to hear ninety-nine positive comments and one negative, and then fixate on the negative which is diminishing to their power.

This brings to mind a client Sarah had. She spoke to a group of 1,500 people and got a standing ovation. She received evaluations back with 1,499 glowing, positive comments, such as "fantastic," "fabulous," "brilliant..." And, she received one negative comment! The author of the comment said, "Your outfit is unprofessional and I don't like your hair."

The client then fixated on the dissenting evaluation, wondering if she should change her look to satisfy the author of the negative comment. Sarah told her "some people come to the planet to be offended and it is impossible to make that one person happy. If you did, you would probably not satisfy the other 1,499."

Keep a journal of all the positive comments people say about you and your leadership.

We partnered on a project with a client. He had a good sized company and asked us to help him grow it. One of our tasks was to interview his employees to see how they felt about him as a leader. He was sure that this would come back as all negatives. We were quite surprised when in fact, the interviews came back ninety-nine percent positive.

He, like many of us, focused on what he saw as shortcomings and disregarded his strengths and achievements. It's as if we have blinders on us about what we either do or have done well. This may develop in childhood or school. However, just because it became a habit doesn't mean that we have to decide to hold onto it.

What we found when clients exploit their strengths is that most of their shortcomings tend to fall away. Therefore, the Magic Mirror is essential as a tool for your leadership growth.

There are, in addition to gaining confidence with your Magic Mirror, tools to become a successful leader. We call these tools the North Star Zone, which are things that will catapult you forward as a leader. By using your North Star

Zone, you will have a straighter path to your success.

Exercise

The first secret of the North Star Zone is your Significant Values. In order to identify these, choose five people you admire. What qualities or characteristics do they have that you respect? Once you have done that, write down why you admire those characteristics. Then, write down some values that you think are important to you from the following list or whatever you can imagine on your own.

Family	Integrity	Kindness
Learning	Self-care	Compassion
Respect	Fairness	Having fun
Inspiration	Creativity	Innovation
Drive	Humor	Generosity
Enthusiasm	Efficiency	Success
Teamwork	Ambition	Gratefulness
Serenity	Trust	Wisdom
Passion	Bravery	Confidence
Making a Difference	Persistence	Responsibility

From all these different sources, whittle down your Significant Values to not more than 20. Now, go back and cross out any you can do without. Now, work that list down to no more than seven. Then, rank them in order of priority from top priority number one to lesser priority of number seven. Use your Significant Values as a compass when making important decisions, when evaluating choices, and helping you to know you are not making serious mistakes.

The second secret of the North Star Zone is Meaningful View. To best explain what this means, imagine you are sitting in the driver's seat and you have no idea where you are going. You might feel stuck because you don't know your destination. You might drive in circles or run into all sorts of dangerous obstacles. You have a greater likelihood of getting where you want to go if you know where you are going. Therefore, to be a better leader, you must create a Meaningful View. To prevent the mishaps from happening, you have to clarify your most important destination of all the possible options. In order to do this, pick a time frame, such as one year, three years, or five years. Now imagine the outcome you want. Describe that outcome in as great a detail as possible. That is your Meaningful View.

_____
_____
_____
_____
_____

Paint a picture in your mind. When Donna first worked with Linda, she had 3 children under five years old and had a small, struggling law practice. As Linda helped her describe her Meaningful View, Donna saw an organized business, time for her family, and hitting the target of a million dollar revenue in less than one year. With Linda's help, she was able to achieve those goals in less than ten months and it all started because she had a Meaningful View.

The third secret of the North Star Zone is Purposeful Quest. Ask yourself what is your cause or calling? Why do you want to achieve your goals?

_____

_____

_____

_____

_____

Once you answer these questions you will know why you should devote the energy to accomplishing your goal as a leader. As an example, Linda worked with a realtor who felt that her purpose was to bring together families around beautiful homes to create safe and happy communities. Sarah worked with a speaker who wanted to change the world by reaching millions of people. That purpose kept the speaker on track until he was able to achieve that goal. When things are tough or you feel confused the Purposeful Quest helps keep you on track.

The fourth secret is Specialization. Consider very carefully what it is you do. As an example, let us say you work in some area of the dental field. This could be selling toothpaste, being a dentist, a hygienist or creating advertisements for a dental association. These are all part of the dental field, but each is special, and different from the other. By having this clarity about your exact niche it informs your behavior. There is less likely to be wasted effort, missteps, or missed opportunities if you have specialization.

When Linda begins working with a new client, it is clear that the client is often unclear about their objective and does not have a defined understanding of the specific nature of her business or offerings. In other words, what is your company meaning, why do you exist, what are you doing in the marketplace? As someone in the financial industry, do you offer planning, coaching, products, etc.? As a Human Resource consultant, do you offer .in-house training, products, leadership development, etc.?

The Purposeful Quest combined with Specialization gives you laser focus.

One of Sarah's clients was speaking on Sales and Leadership to anyone who could fog a mirror and had a pulse with varying degrees of success. When the client switched to his specialization to helping people in the healthcare arena working with nurses, his business quadrupled.

Leadership in large part is having a quality that helps us to influence others. If we don't believe in ourselves, we cannot expect others to follow us. Confidence is communicated certainly with words and actions. However, using some of the techniques presented in this chapter provides you with a strong sense of your own skills and abilities. That, in turn, gives you confidence, which creates stronger leadership. Let's learn more about developing confidence.

Chapter Two

Confidence for Action

Seeing your true value gives you power to lead others. However, you must have confidence and maintain your confidence for taking action. There is an intellectual awareness based on degrees, certificates, awards, accolades and experience. There is also an emotional awareness that powers action. You must activate that emotional awareness in order to move forward with confidence.

A client that Sarah worked with had been around the world, had two bestselling books, thousands in crowds who cheered for her and she had won every award you can possibly imagine. On the evening she was about to get the biggest award in her industry; she turned to Sarah and said, "I don't know why they're giving this to me. There are so many people who deserve it more."

Even though the world recognized her brilliance, she still didn't connect emotionally to her achievements. In order to actively contribute to those you lead, you must make the connection between intellectual and emotional awareness.

Exercise

Let's list all the things you have accomplished and achieved, and imagine that they had happened to someone else. Be sure to write down even the smallest of these. What would you say about that person? How would you feel about that person? What would you tell them to do? This will build the emotional connection to your strengths which, will in turn, make you more powerful.

_____

_____

_____

_____

_____

Another strategy to build your confidence actually has two parts. First, imagine the most confident person you can think of. Imagine them standing behind a door. Imagine the door opens from floor to ceiling slowly. Imagine their feet, their knees, their waist, their shoulders, their hand, their face, their hair.

Next, imagine you are that person behind the door. Walk into their body and take on what they're wearing, how they are moving, tilt of their head and the confidence on their face. Do you feel more confident?

Another way to do this is to choose someone who you greatly admire, and when you look at them, you often wish you could be like. It could be a person you know, television personality, or a movie character. Once you have chosen this person, especially when you want to feel confident, envision yourself as this other person. It helps to imagine pulling a cloak over yourself and taking on that persona.

Another client of ours was a leader of a large organization and would have panic attacks every time she was going to speak to all of her employees. When she took on the character of the confident person, she changed the way she dressed, the way she stood and walked, and even breathed with more confidence. This is similar to what Beyoncé does when she creates her onstage character of Sasha Fierce.

These types of actions can evoke a very fast transition. In addition to changing your thoughts as we suggested above, there are some other techniques that can be equally effective. As an example, what you wear, the language you choose, and the tone and volume of your voice can be used to enhance your power.

Surprisingly, one of the top questions Sarah gets asked by her clients is "What do I wear if I want to look powerful?" She tells them that with our culture getting more casual with clothing, it is hard to know what to wear, but some things can make a big difference. For men, a simple addition of a sport coat makes him look more professional.

There's a famous story about President Washington, our Founding Father, which says that he was not exactly a shoo-in for president when our country was being formed. His wife was concerned that his outfits didn't lend people to think of him as presidential. She made him an outfit with shoulder pads and epaulets that looked like a top general's outfit. As the story goes, people then began to take him more seriously in his new outfit and this was one element that lead them to choose him as President.

We are trained to think of shoulder pads and a man's jacket as being more powerful than a t-shirt.

With women, color is key. Choosing reds, royal blues, emerald greens – vibrant colors – can make you come across as the onstage expert.

There is a wonderful book called Casual Power by Sherry Maysonave, where she talks about men and women's casual clothing options if they want to maintain their power. It includes many pictures and drawings to explain what to do.

Your word choice can make a big difference in how you are perceived. Language can elicit emotion. Using language such as "I choose to do something "is more empowering than "I have to do something," "I'm in demand" is more empowering than "I'm overwhelmed." Words like "I think" "maybe" "possibly" "just my idea" are disempowering.

Using a negative point of view also diminishes your power. Some examples are, "I don't want to mess this up" versus "this will go well." "They probably think I'm stupid" versus "perhaps I'm not being understood."

It is also true that volume and tone, makes a difference in how you come across. If you walk into a room and see someone yelling, it might strike fear into some, but it won't create loyalty which is one of the components of true power. If someone speaks in an extremely quiet voice they are perceived as not being powerful. In fact, that may make the listener feel as if that person is timid.

Tone is also important. If the speaker sounds like Minnie Mouse, they will be perceived as child-like. More resonant voices like the famed actor, James Earl Jones, the voice of CNN and Star War's Darth Vader, are perceived as powerful. If you want to have a better tone to your voice there are exercises you can do.

One exercise you can do is called intoning and it is something that actors do. Take a book and begin reading in a chant like fashion. Do it until you can feel vibrations in your face. Make sure that you are breathing from your belly and not your chest. Sit up straight and keep your shoulders relaxed. This will make you more resonant and your voice more powerful.

We have talked about ways to increase your confidence. Now, let's discuss how to turn that confidence into action.

It is challenging to become a powerful and successful leader. Even though you now feel confident, to be a better leader, an important action to take is to get prepared. The way to start is to evaluate the situation. Then figure out in what way things will be improved. Once you have that information, set your goal. Now you are ready to make a plan.

Exercise

If you could wave a magic wand, where would your business be in five years, three years, or one year? Would your profits be up by 75%? Would your business have grown to twice its size? Would your productivity be increased by 25%? Work backwards from 5 years to 3 years to 1 year – what would you have to begin doing now to reach those goals?

5 years

_____

_____

_____

3 years

_____

_____

_____

1 year

_____

_____

_____

First talk to anyone you think might have information about what you plan to do, such as someone who is in the field already and more advanced than you. Capture those ideas below and leave that alone for at least a week. Then write down your thoughts about what you discovered with no editing or judgment. Just spill forth whatever comes to mind. Once that is done, go back and strike out what doesn't seem right to you. Then, go back and do that again. What you have left is likely to be important and meaningful. Then, number each item on your list by priority. That can be how much you like the idea or by how valuable you deem it to be. Now, assign a deadline for each item and get started. Ideas:

_____

_____

_____

_____

_____

What you Discovered:

_____

_____

_____

_____

_____

Priority List: Deadline:

_____

_____

_____

_____

_____

Confidence can be very helpful in your leadership role at work or perhaps when you are out networking. However, the next logical step to exercise that confidence is to be influential with others. Now is when you take another form of action, whether that action is to conduct a better company meeting, rally the troupes, or connect with new possible business partners.

Leaders throughout the ages have strived to influence others. Obviously, confidence is very important; however you can have confidence and still not influence in the way you want.

As a leader, you will need to influence a Board of Directors, employees, customers or clients, or power partners.

It is very important to empower others. When Linda owned her company, some of her employees were laborers whose attitude was that they come to work, spend the hours, and collect a paycheck. Linda wanted them to take ownership in the care of their trucks, in their safety on the road, and with customers at the docks. Even though she wanted to give them training, her first step was to engage them by asking what they thought needed to be improved or how they could help the company to be better. Their attitudes and even demeanors changed completely because they felt that their thoughts and actions would make a difference.

Some leaders are tempted to use force. There is a big difference between force and influence. Force gives you temporary positive results but in the long run only true power and influence can be sustained. If you demonstrate the behavior you want to see in others, you will have greater influence. You have to be the role model. If you don't display the qualities you look for in others, no matter what you say or do, and how much confidence you have, you won't be able to move people to the behavior you want.

Exercise

What five qualities would you like to see in your employees? How can you demonstrate those qualities in your business life? For example, if you want more loyalty from your employees, how can you demonstrate more loyalty to them?

_____

_____

_____

_____

_____

A wonderful book on the psychology of influence is called, "Influence" by Cialdini. We highly recommend that you read this book if you want to be more influential.

Since we understand the value of having confidence, instilling confidence in others is very powerful. A good way to do that is to put yourself in someone else's shoes. Sometimes, it is difficult to relate to another person if our experiences and circumstances are vastly different.

Linda had an employee that she liked very much. She admired his work ethic and his attitude. In addition, she noticed that he was very well-liked by others. One of her standards for her employees was to come to work on time. This man always came late. She felt disturbed by this one issue. She talked to him several times and he seemed a little ashamed, but never offered a reason explanation. After several warnings, reluctantly she told him he would either have to start coming on time or she would have no choice but to let him go. Those were the magic words because he then explained what was going on.

He had recently moved to the United States from another country. His wife worked and had to be at work at a certain time and his children needed to be driven to school. He felt that the neighborhood he lived in wasn't safe enough to let them go to school on their own. So in order to drive them, he would have to come late to work.

After Linda heard this explanation, she indeed put herself into his shoes and felt she would do the same thing in those circumstances. For a short time, she allowed him to come in a little late, while he saved up the money for a second car so his wife could drive his children to school and herself to work.

This created such loyalty and he did such an exceptional job that he was eventually promoted to plant manager.

By putting herself in his place, she got an invaluable employee.

Another way to take action to instill confidence in others is to focus on and highlight the best qualities of those you lead.

Have you ever noticed a change in how you feel having just received a compliment? Usually, we feel a slight lift in our mood. Can you imagine if you focus on the best qualities of people who work for you or those you seek to influence? If you want to influence certain behavior in others, this is a successful strategy. As an example, Sarah had a client who realized that she wasn't acknowledging her staff and was only focusing on the negatives. She decided to put five pennies in her right pocket and to transfer one to her left pocket every time she acknowledged someone on her staff. At the end of each day she had to have moved all five pennies to her left pocket. The result was that productivity went up and loyalty and enthusiasm went through the roof.

Whether you want to build your own confidence or boost the confidence of others, you must use techniques to make that happen. Be sure to keep motivated and stay aware of your own behavior. Take notice of the effect your changes have made.

As a Leader, it is helpful to know for yourself and for others how to reach the success we all seek. For overall success, we offer our 4-Part Formula to achieve absolutely anything:

There are really only 4 qualities anyone needs to make a business work, reach your goal at work or achieve most anything you can dream. Here is the magic formula to make most anything happen:

1. **Desire/Passion**
   a. You must have an unstoppable, driving desire to get what you want; nothing less will do.
   b. You must have an unyielding passion to do what you want to do.

2. **Belief** - you can want something very badly, and can have a passion for doing it – and still not *believe* you can do it. As an example, someone can very badly want to be an actress; she can have a passion for doing it. However, she must also believe she can be an actress and succeed at doing it.

3. **Resources**
   a. Ability to find resources – You must find what you need to make what you want happen. As an example, as a business owner, Linda needed to know how to purchase a scrap metal truck – which was different from other trucks. She had to find people, who could tell her about

finding this kind of truck, look online for an answer, visit truck dealers, etc. You have to have the ability to find the resources to get what you want.

b. Ability to implement resources – Once you find a resource, you must find a way to implement or use the resource. As an example, if one of your resources is the HR firm for your company, you must decide what services it offers that work for your purposes.

4. **Persistence** – Everyone falls down from time to time. You must be able to get up, dust yourself off, and get back into the game. If you quit, you lose; you don't achieve.

"Never, never, never, never give up!"

Winston Churchill

Chapter Three

How to Win with Processes and Systems

Linda has observed that many of her clients get stuck in the planning stage. Planning, although it requires some degree of creativity is actually more fun and feels easier than coming up with the "how-to" to achieve that plan.

It's easier to dream of an outcome than to figure out how to make it come true. Therefore, you must be highly motivated to do the work required to either identify or develop systems and processes. Even more difficult is the "doing" or the implementation and execution of the plan.

However, the thrill of activating a plan and especially the joy of creating the outcome you desired seems well worth the effort.

So let's start with the easy part, planning.

Most people when they first decide to go into business, that decision is usually generated because another family member had a similar business, because you were trained in a specific area, or you discovered you had a particular talent or skill. The problem that arises is that many people do not have business training.

They may be great at lawn care or making doughnuts, and may have done a fabulous job working for someone else. When it is time for you to win clients and make a profit, their lack of business training becomes apparent.

Yet, that problem can be overcome by some basic and relatively easy processes and systems.

Step One: Company Meaning

Have a complete understanding of why you are in business. Why does your business exist? Is there a particular cause that is important to you that made you want to start your business? How is the world better off because your business exists? In other words, how will your company improve the world, make it a better place, increase the quality of life, right a wrong, or prevent the end from coming to something good? You replied to some of these questions in Chapter One.

You must clearly identify your purpose for being in business. See if you can distinguish your company from other companies that do the same thing that you do.

Step Two: Identify your Company Core Values

Usually when two people get married, they have often been attracted by common values. Without those, there usually is not a firm foundation from which choices and decisions can be made. The same is very true for a business.

Refer back to your Significant Values in Chapter One.

Now, if you have employees, call a meeting and let them know that you are choosing company core values. Get their input. Do the same thing here as you did in Chapter One. Your goal is to narrow your list down to five to seven values. Even though, this process of choosing company core values may be challenging because your employees' viewpoints may differ with your opinions and each other's opinions, if everyone understands that the purpose of doing this is to help the company to be healthy and to grow, making your final choices can be accomplished.

Once you have about 10-20 values on your list, cross-out those that you can all agree are a little less important than others. Continue doing that until you have the number that you need.

It's important to post your values where everyone in your company can see them as well as on your company website. When you first hire a person, you show him or her your Significant Value list. Have a discussion with your new hire and advise him or her that it is necessary for him or her to share those values. Make sure that you get verbal and written agreement that your new employee shares these values.

You can use the following form when you are first hiring someone or it is advised to use it as well in your monthly, quarterly, or yearly employee evaluations.

Employee Name _____   Rate 1 to 10

Honesty	8
Kindness	3
Punctuality	7
Teamwork	5
Making a Difference	6
Creativity	6
Trust	8

If the potential employee has less than a "7" in "3" or more values, it would be unadvisable to hire him or her. Have questions prepared that will elicit responses that will allow you to evaluate their true values. For instance, "Tell me a time when you worked on a team and you experienced a challenge" or "are there any organizations or charities that you believe in?" or "What would you do if you heard people gossiping about someone at work?"

As daily decisions are made about process, systems, policies, communication, proposals, etc., there must be a time when there is a planned evaluation to make certain that all the things that you are doing are fitting with your values.

Without matching your values, one person can take down your whole company. For example, a salesperson you hire is great at getting sales, but lacks integrity; he could ruin the entire reputation of your business.

Step Three: Vision and Entrepreneurial Mantra.

Vision: As we said earlier, if you get into a car without knowing the location you want to reach and if you didn't have tools like a gas pedal and break, you would just sit there or go around in circles. With a Business Vision you know, at least, where you want to go. You have to ask yourself where you want to be in the future – in one year, in three years, in ten years - in terms of your business. Do you want to be in a certain kind of building or office? Do you want a certain number of employees? Do you want to be known for a special result you deliver?

At this point, do not include a financial projection. We'll get to that soon. For our purposes, you just want a firm idea, something short that solidifies what you see as the future of your business. This is not a process to use if you are planning to construct a business plan to secure a business loan from a bank. That kind of business plan is generated to impress the bankers. This just requires a few sentences or about one paragraph.

An Entrepreneurial Mantra: Once you have your Company Meaning set, the next step is to write an Entrepreneurial Mantra, which is something a phrase or words one repeats believed to have some psychological or spiritual power. Linda's company mantra is "Striving toward greatness" because she believes that   is what she helps her clients, who are business owners and professionals, do. Sarah's   company mantra is "Do Something Brave Every Day."

Use your company meaning to develop a mantra which must be no more than 3 to 5 words. If you know the essence of your company, you can play around with words until you feel you have captured in your mantra the expression of the reason you have a company.

At this point, you want to display your Company Meaning, Core Values, and Mantra.

When you are making decisions for your company, go back to those core company principles to make sure you are making the right decisions.

As previously stated, you do not need a thick, 50-page business plan to get your business on track. Instead, you can accomplish your goals by creating a One-page Business Plan, which includes your Vision, Mission, Objectives, Strategies, and Actions. We've already talked about your Vision so let's move on to your Mission.

Step Four: Company Mission

This is similar to your Company Meaning, however, we like to have our clients do both. Your mission talks, in a general sense, about how you will accomplish your vision. As an example, Sarah's company, The Victory Company, has a mission of "Double your business, double your impact, change the world. "Linda's company, Optimal Level, has a mission of "We take businesses from where they are to where they want to be."

A few other examples are Walt Disney: *Happiest celebration on earth*, Nike: *To bring inspiration and innovation to every athlete in the world* and Wal-Mart: *Saving people money so they can live better.*

Step Five: Your Objectives

You may have different objectives for your business, but for our purposes, I would like to focus on your financial objective. What is the gross amount (earnings before taxes and expenses) of money, you want or need to earn from your business for the next year? We will call that your financial objective.

After you have set your financial objective, you need to have a Menu of Offerings. Let's use a dog sitting service as an example. If your financial objective is $50, 000 per year, how much do you charge per hour per dog? Let's say you charge $10 per hour, how many dogs would you need to sit to equal $50,000 per year? Let's say that you watched dogs on Saturdays and Sundays too. (Likely you would charge more on the week-ends.) Let's say you watched the dogs for only 8 hours a day.

8 hours x 365 = 2, 920 hours a year x $10 per hour = $29, 200 per year. You might have to charge more on the week-ends or add services to reach your goal.

The point is that for your business, you might just have a few options, as an example, coaching. A coach might just offer 3 to 5 programs. Someone who is a graphic designer would have to choose from several design options to identify all her offerings and what is charged for those offerings.

But, that is what is necessary deciding on your menu of offerings and determining the cost for each to see how many clients/customers you need to reach your desired gross income.

Step Six: Marketing Strategies

Now that we know how many clients (we'll use this term to also mean customers) we need to make our desired income for a year, we have to decide how we will get those customers. That means, we have to begin marketing.

Before we do that, you need to do the following:

1. Identify your ideal customer/client – age, industry, geographic location, interests, likes, habits, challenges they face for which you provide a solution, etc.

2. Figure out what makes your company unique; this is similar to brand. Understand your

Unique Selling Proposition. According to Wikipedia, that is a term used to refer to any aspect of an object that differentiates it from similar objects. Basically, it is what in your opinion differentiates you and your product or service.

Imagine there are two dry cleaners on the same street on an intersection across from one another. Green Cleaners has coffee and tea and pastries whenever you come in. They remember your name, your kid's names and your grandchildren's names – and they treat you like family. Blue Cleaners is all about speed and they get your order out in a day. They also have a terrific onsite tailor. Even though each dry cleaner does primarily the same thing, and are near each other, they attract different clientele.

When you are looking for your Unique Selling Proposition, you do not have to be different from your competition, you just have to find what makes you distinct. Let us say you are a financial advisor and you are thinking about what makes you unique. Here is an example of two different financial advisors and how they are distinct. Mr. Brown has very large corporate clients, is extremely efficient and highly knowledgeable about intricate financial situations, and works in a high rise downtown. Mr. Yellow makes house calls, makes people feel special, and works with individual rather than corporate accounts. If you focus on your values, your company meaning, your vision and mission, you will get a picture of what is amazing about you and your company.

There are any number of marketing strategies. You can go online and type in "marketing strategies" in the subject line and you will find many choices. Some examples are *Networking, Expos, Speaking, Social Media, Content Marketing [writing blogs, articles, white papers, etc.], referral marketing, and lumpy packages [things of unusual size and shape that can be sent directly to the client that they will enjoy.]*

Marketing means going to market; using strategies and processes to sell a product or service, to bring customers to you, to make prospects aware of the benefits of using your product or service. There are three ways to grow your business:

1. Acquiring more customers
2. Persuading each customer to buy more products or services
3. Persuading each customer to buy more expensive or profitable products or services

Some marketing strategies are more expensive than others. Most small business owners do not have a lot of money for marketing. In that case, choose marketing strategies such as the 3-foot rule (which means talking to anyone within 3 feet of you at any given time), networking, or blogging.

Step Seven: Choose Your Actions

Once you know your 5 top marketing strategies, you are ready for the next part of your one-page business plan which is Actions. At this point, you want to determine which actions you will take to execute your marketing strategies.

This brings us to sales and we will get to that in Section Two of this book.

Step Eight: Plans for employees

You need to know how to hire the right people for your jobs. So first, you need to have job descriptions as you take on employees. It is imperative that you identify the roles that you want your employees to hold.

You need excellent processes for hiring the right people to fill those roles. To do that, use your core values and as you interview your new hires, see if they will fit these values. As you continue to grow your company, you develop a company culture. Part of hiring well is determining if the person you are considering for the job fits your company culture.

Also, determine if a new hire genuinely understands all aspects of your job including hours, responsibilities, company structure, etc. Determine if she wants the job, has the skills that are necessary to do the job, or the intellect and personality required.

If you are just starting out or have a very small company, you may need to think about finding part-time people to help you grow. We call this Situation-Solution hiring. For example, if the situation you have is that you don't have to do all of your bookkeeping, a bookkeeper is an obvious solution. If you need things picked up and dropped in the afternoon, a neighboring high-school kid may be the solution to the situation. A stay-at-home mom who works on an "as needed" basis may be the solution to the 10 hours a week when you need extra help, but she may be able to disappear when times are slow.

It has become more common for small business owners to hire outside contractors. According to Google, Independent Contractors are "business owners, and are not their clients' employees. They do not receive employee benefits or the same **legal** protections as employees, and are often responsible for their **own** expenses."

Often people tend to think that they need to wait until they are large enough to hire a full-time person when a combination of part-time and Virtual Assistants maybe more effective and help you grow faster sooner. Make a list of the all the situations you need help with and get creative with the solutions.

Step Nine: Plans for Operations

Linda has seen her clients get overwhelmed as their company grew. Of course, there are many times when a business owner will get overwhelmed. However, there are, at least, three main parts to operational plans that will likely make every day at work easier for the business owner.

One is being aware of primary, pressing issues. Linda once had a client who had a plumbing company. When she started working with them, the company was about three years old. They were growing in terms of employees and profits. However, they felt confused about how to move forward and exactly what they were doing. Linda helped them identify the specific issues that were causing the problem.

For one thing, they did not have any processes, for another the owner of the company was doing both the client work out in the field as well as managing the company. Linda had to find a solution so that strategy and oversight were the main focus for the owner. In order to do that, Linda helped him to develop better training programs for his employees, to create a budget, and to start a time-management system for himself. The result was turn over dropped down, efficiency went way up, and the owner had peace of mind.

The second part is overcoming the feeling that one's business is spiraling out of control and the third is measuring your progress.

Most often, business owners take on clients and employees without identifying processes. This is true for professionals, as well, who focus on solving every day, immediate challenges having originally neglected to set up systems and processes. The solution is to identify the steps being taken, give the process a name, and then save it in one place along with other processes as you develop them.

Everybody in the company or organization needs to be given those processes even if they are not a direct part of that process.

The third necessary element to operational sanity is to make sure that you are measuring your progress. That could be financial, sales success, or employee's problems. Therefore, in addition to gaining control of your issues and processes, you have to create ways to evaluate the systems that you have put in place. Why continue using a system that may not be helping you produce the best results. That is why, you constantly – and that means weekly – need to read your numbers to inform you if you are possibly losing money or sales, spending too much money or spending it in the wrong way or if you are not taking care of your current clients or customers in the best way possible.

A good leader listens to his employees, customers, associates, etc. to identify problem areas and to get new ideas. Then, a leader can consult with the right people to find the information to formulate solutions.

If you try to do it all alone, you will fail. If you try to use the old-fashioned dictatorial style of forcing your ideas on those around you, you will fail. If you do not track progress and make adjustments, you will fail.

A good leader uses suggestions from those around him or her to identify those issues that need to be addressed. Sometimes just the act of tracking can give you the information that you need.

One of Linda's clients wanted to be a good boss. Before he started his own company, he worked for a manufacturer. So he knew some of the shortcomings leaders often have because he worked for someone who was less than ideal. He wanted to be understanding and sympathetic.

He had one employee that he kept making excuses for. However, once he created his Core Company Values and tracked his employee's performance, he had to acknowledge a problem.

Then, because he had a system of communicating to his employees areas that needed improvement, he was able to set boundaries and track the outcome. Without waiting too long, he realized he had to fire this employee. After that, he began feeling happier, his employees seemed grateful and there was a better atmosphere all around, and the new employee he hired was eager, enthusiastic, and quite good at what he did. Overall the company went on to be much more successful.

Another client was actually generating lots of business, but was losing money. How could that be? As a good leader, she needed to take a hard look at her systems. Once she did that, she discovered that she had given too many concessions with her proposals, had lost track of time involved in job completions, and had not been on top of lost revenue. Once she began having weekly meetings and developing processes to capture that data, everything began to change for the better.

In terms of leaders winning by using processes and systems, they must become aware of how that which they are responsible for is being organized. They must ask themselves and others what is not working and what steps do they need to take to change that. Being aware and taking action must be ongoing and if one stops being diligent, problems multiply.

Step Ten: Successful Time Management

There may be two extremes when it comes to choosing whether or not to take care of something by yourself or to engage others. Similar to juggling too many balls until it is impossible and they all fall down, when a leader attempts to do everything there is to do by his or herself, catastrophe can happen. On the other hand, if a leader – either because of insecurity or lack of trust in his or her own knowledge, chooses to hire too many people inside and outside of the company, he or she may be blowing the budget and or abdicating too much power. Each decision requires a lot of thought. When making this decision, check yourself to see if you are falling on either side of the extreme.

In order to be a good leader, you must be in control of your time. Our Time Container system is very helpful in gaining mastery of your time. We have observed many of our clients, who were talented in their areas of expertise, who suffer the consequences of not having good control of their time. When you are leading others, the demands on you are great. Even if you have a practice or are a solopreneur, you wear different hats and can neglect important parts of your life or business if you fail to be in command of your time.

Our Time Container system will give you clarity about how and when you spend your time. This system has been known to free up more than ten hours a week in productive time for leaders. One example of this is Jane, one of our clients. In addition to running her own business, she was also the President of a national organization. When she came to us, she was frazzled and overwhelmed and losing many hours of productivity a week. After learning the Time Container System, she was saving 14 ½ hours a week and gained more time for work planning, client acquisition, and a personal life. She even lost some weight because she no longer speeding through McDonalds but had time to take better care of herself.

Container System

If you think about it, you can actually assign a category of activity to everything you do in your daily life. For instance, going to the drugstore is actually a personal chore. Going to events to prospect for clients is networking. Planning to help your employees do better at something can be classified as Strategy. Therefore, you can break down all of your activities into categories.

Step 1 - For a period of two weeks, keep a record of everything you do during your work hours. Some people work until ten at night, some people are through at 5 p.m. Your work hours start when you start working and end when you stop.

Here is a sample list of categories: Marketing, Sales, Production (anything you are doing for your client) Strategy (thinking and planning) Travel, Networking, Self- Care (eating, shower, getting your hair done, making meals, etc.) Meetings (Administration, Sales, etc.)

Step 2 – Your record will include the activity you are doing, category into which it fits, Start time and End time, and a running total of time.

Step 3 – Keep a running record of each category and how much time you spend doing each activity. So, you might have 20 hours for the category of Travel in two weeks. You might have 4 or 5 hours for Strategy in two weeks. You might have 10 hours for Personal Care and so forth.

Activity	Category	Start time	End time	Total Time
Travel to client	Travel	9:00 a.m.	9:30 a.m.	30.00
Client meeting	Production	9:30 a.m.	10:30 a.m.	60.00
Travel to office	Travel	10:30 a.m.	11:00 a.m.	30.00
Visit school for son	Personal chore	11:00 a.m.	11:15 a.m.	15:00
Drive to restaurant	Travel	11:15 a.m.	11:30 a.m.	15.00
Lunch	Self-care	11:30 a.m.	12:00 p.m.	30.00
Work on project	Production	12:00 p.m.	1:00 p.m.	60.00
Meet with vendor	Administration	1:00 p.m.	1:40 p.m.	40.00
Meet with manager	Administration	1:40 p.m.	2:00 p.m.	20.00
Prospect meeting	Sales	2:00 p.m.	4:00 p.m.	120.00
Work on core values	Strategy	4:00 p.m.	5:00 p.m.	60.00
Travel to event	Travel	5:00 p.m.	5:30 p.m.	30.00
Chamber event	Networking	5:30 p.m.	7:00 p.m.	90.00

Daily Total Hours 600.00

10 hours

Step 4 – Total all the work hours for your two weeks. An example is "100 hours in 2 weeks."

Step 5 – Total the number of hours by category. Add them to the containers below.

Step 6 – Translate each number into percentages for the whole two weeks. For example, if you spent 10 hours on networking in two weeks that would be 10 percent of the total. Enter your percentages into that space on your bucket.

Step 7 – Now, analyze your data. How does it look to you? Do you have too much travel time, not enough sales time, etc.? What would you ideally like your pie chart to look like? Play around with your time containers until you they are where you would ideally like them to be.

Step 8 – Try out your new Time Container system. Keep notes as these will change for a while until you feel comfortable and have the best control of your time.

Step 9 - After about a month, you should have a good idea about how to divide your time. Now, using a color-coded system, place your activity container categories on your calendar. This can be done on a paper or electronic calendar.

There will be times when you cannot keep your commitment to do that activity at that time. That's fine. However, you can borrow from another time from your calendar to make sure that percentages are balanced. For example if something comes up during your Strategy Time that is a Sales opportunity, you can plug your Strategy Time into one of your Sales times.

	Monday	Tuesday	Wednesday	Thursday	Friday
9 a.m.	Meeting w/Employees	Engineer Assoc.	Strategy Breakfast	Work on	CRM
9:30	Travel to Prospect	Meet w/Bill Jones from XY Smith Co.	Sales Meeting with Bill Peterson	Meeting w/ Service Mgr.	Meet w/Plane
10:00	Sales Call	Sales Call	Meet with Business Coach	Travel time	Travel Time
10:30				Appt. w/Vet	
11:00	Bring car in for service	Meeting w/ Dawn Utley	Travel to Chicago	Sales Call	Work on Evening Event
11:15	Chamber Lunch	Meeting w/Bob Kaplan	Bring the car in for service	Meeting w/ Account list	
12:00					Meet w/Don Alexander
12:15	Travel to Prospect	Meeting with Plant Manager	ACA Luncheon	Travel to Restaurant	

The Importance of Continual Learning:

It is common for business owners to feel bogged down by everyday activities and pressures. However, we have to have a broader view. There are, at least, two main reasons to become a life-long learner. One is that when you do pull yourself away to read a book, attend a seminar, listen to a podcast, find a coach, etc., you may feel a new sense of confidence and may be refreshed and ready to approach issues from a different point of view. Also, what you have learned will be of benefit to your employees.

Section Two
Sales

Chapter Four

Win-win Sales

Have you ever had a revelation? Well, Linda once had a revelation about sales. The very first day that she went out to sell scrap metal services, she discovered that the factory she was in had only plastic scrap. She was about to turn and leave, when the owner of the company asked if she would like to see a tour of the plant.

During the tour, she had her revelation. She imagined a boy on the ground playing with stick figures. Then, envisioned a man seeing that scene and thinking I can make those toys so much better using plastic.

Linda thought of this man as a visionary. Then, she realized that he would need an engineer to design the figures, machines to make them, machinists to run the machines, a building to house them, and realtors and attorneys to make the transactions and eventually administrative staff.

Then, she saw stacks of shelves with these toys on them. These toys would just be sitting there without someone to make the connection between these toys and the child.

That's where the sales person comes in. Without the sales person absolutely nothing happens.

We see this position as honorable and one that helps business flourish.

Sarah often says that sales are the graceful art of helping other people get what they truly want.

Unfortunately, because of what dates back to the shifty snake-oil salesman, people hold on to the mistaken idea that a sales person is unscrupulous and intends to force someone to do something they don't want to do or cheat someone out of money.

Good sales are nothing further away from that concept. Sales are making a connection between someone who may need or want something of great value with someone who has a product or service that is valued.

The result of a transaction between these two parties is something positive and dates back to caveman days. In early days, one caveman would say to the other "I have a goat and I would like to buy your pelt." How about my goat for your pelt?"

What he didn't say was, "let me show you my Power Point presentation about my goat."

It was goat for pelt, pelt for goat, meaning each had something the other one wanted and they were able to exchange.

Sometimes we forget that we are simply trying to find people who need what we have, as sales people.

Therefore, let's not get confused and worry that our as salespeople we must take advantage of anyone. Instead, it is honorable and win-win.

Getting people to buy from you:

In all our years of helping our clients, we have noticed that many people are frustrated that their potential buyers don't get how fantastic their product or service is; especially when they take the time to go on and on and explain it in great detail. This is a serious problem for anyone wanting to convert a prospect into a buyer.

All the crying and screaming about how a product or service does cartwheels and has great fireworks will not make the prospect change his or her mind. Instead, the sales person must change her focus to what the prospect wants. This is important because when someone is in the midst of a sales presentation, it is difficult to see clearly what exactly is going on.

The bells and whistles do not matter to a prospect. What does matter is their own needs, wants, concerns, issues, frustrations, goal, dreams, desires, etc. Therefore, what a seller must focus on are those things first. Once you have this information, you can show how your product or service provides a solution or satisfies those needs. Now, it will be easier to have your prospect buy from you.

The Dance: Being in control of the sale

Just like in ballroom dancing, someone must lead. Often it is the man. By putting his hand at the woman's lower back, and both joining hands, he can gracefully guide across the floor so that both dancers feel comfortable and sure. When the leader fails to guide strongly and isn't in control of the other person, a lot can go wrong...toes get stepped on, embarrassment may occur because it looks and feels like both people are going in different directions, and on occasion some people may fall to the floor.

Therefore, both parties appreciate when someone leads. The same is true for a sales situation. The prospective buyer is comfortable with the sales person directing the conversation and the result is best for both people.

Chapter Five

Don't Try to Win Them All

Sarah once had a client who came to her in tears saying that she was upset because there were certain people that would just not buy from her. Sarah asked, "What percentage of people are not buying from you?"

She replied, "20 percent! Isn't that terrible?" Sarah said, "Actually you are selling 80% of the people who come to you and that is great."

Do you want to marry every person on earth? Do you want to see every movie? Do you want to buy every house? Of course not!

Obviously, we are exaggerating. However, the point is people are mostly attracted based on who they are and how they fit with a product of service.

Salespeople need to focus on the people who want to buy from them rather than those who don't.

The number one problem we see with sales people is that they don't talk to enough people so that those percentages can come out favorably for them.

Then, they don't track the numbers of people to whom they talk in order be able to know their own statistics on how many people they need to contact to have successful sales numbers.

Most people try to pressure three people into buying from them instead of speaking to 50 and discovering that 30 are interested.

We are really in favor of tracking in order to figure out how many people you need to contact in order to meet your sales goals. What you track you tend to attract.

Below is a easy tracking form. You need to adapt the form for your product or service. The idea is to capture the results you've produced based on the actions you took. When you can see how close you came to your goal, you have the data to tweak what you want to do in the future.

Year -
Financial Goal -
# of networking events attended -

Event One
____ # of phone calls made
____ # of contacts made
____ # of appointments made
____ # of closed sales

Event Two
____ # of phone calls made
____ # of contacts made
____ # of appointments made
____ # of closed sales

Event Three
____ # of phone calls made
____ # of contacts made
____ # of appointments made
____ # of closed sales

A great sales person is like a clever detective. The detective needs to ask a lot of questions to get to the truth. It's the same for a salesperson.

By asking questions we learn about needs, attitudes, desires, fears, confusion, concerns, etc.

Start off with bonding questions that create connection between you and the prospect. Then, ask open-ended probing questions to see if your prospect has a need or wants your product or service. Next ask test-close questions and finally actual closing questions.

Bonding Questions: These questions establish trust between you and the buyer because these queries are about who the person is and what's going on in his or her life. Examples may be, "tell me about what you do, what got you started or what do you like best about what you do?"

Open-ended probing questions: These questions have more to do with a prospect's challenges, needs, or desires. Examples may be: What's most important to you? Describe the problem you are having. How has your service been with your current provider?

Test-close questions: These are questions that move the process forward without necessarily closing the sale immediately. An example may be: What's our next step? Which color would you prefer? How soon do you need this?

Closing questions: These are questions that bring the sale to a close. Examples may be: Should I write up the order today? Shall we get started next Tuesday? Shall we deliver the equipment on Wednesday or Friday?

Chapter Six

Networking your Way to Success

The nature of developing business has dramatically changed in the past 40 years. When Linda started selling in scrap metal business, she could walk right in the front door and ask to speak to a buyer or pick up the phone and get a buyer to talk with her. Now, "no soliciting" is the norm and voice mail screens out your ability to talk to the buyer.

What has become essential is networking. This system of business development has become successful because people want to do business with people they know, like, and trust. What exactly is networking? In its most basic form, it is attending events or meetings to find potential customers or partners who will refer business to you.

In the words of Ivan Misner, Founder of Business Network International, "Networking is the process of developing contacts and relationships to increase your business, enhance your knowledge, expand your sphere of influence, or serve the community. In its most basic form "business networking" is leveraging your business and personal connections to bring you a regular supply of new business."

We have found that many networkers are quite vague about how they go about networking. They seem to show up at a networking event without rhyme or reason about what they are trying to accomplish. How can you get the results you want if you haven't thought about what you want to achieve? You need a working plan.

A good place to start is by identifying who you want to meet. As an example, someone who owns a video company would not want to attend an association of executive assistants. They would not be in the market or the decision makers for purchasing videos. Instead, she would want to attend an association of marketers. Make a list of five potential buyers. Where would those potential buyers congregate? A good way to do this is to use Google. Simply type in the potential buyer type and followed by the word "association." Then, consider distance, cost, and perhaps size of the group. Now, you have a better idea of where to go to find who you're looking for.

Another suggestion is to visit one of your local chamber of commerce meetings. This is a good choice especially if you sell something that anybody can use. If you are a novice networker this is a good choice too. Once you have more experience, you may be able to find more targeted events.

A popular trend is referral or peer-mentoring groups. In most cases, these are started by one or a few people who find they share commonalities. These groups grow with various networking purposes and rules. It is valuable to belong to one these groups because the members become well-connected and actively market for one another. You can search for these organizations in your area, such as the American Club Association, National Association of Women Business Owners, or Young President's Association. Usually, the deeper connections are made by joining and regularly attending committees, boards, or business development groups.

If you work primarily with women, as an example, there are hundreds of women's organizations in every city. Linda once had a client who did independent marketing for repair car shops. She searched for organizations of auto repair shop owners.

Another time, Linda was working with a client who provided consulting to financial firms. When Linda asked her how she was doing finding prospects at her networking events, her client replied that she wasn't meeting anyone who could be a prospect. Linda explained that she needed to go to places where her prospects would be. Her client said that she had no idea where her prospects would be. Then, Linda asked her client to tell her about some of the people in her network. It turned out that one of those people was the president of a bank and another was a CEO. Linda told her client to call them and ask them where they networked. By the time, we finished this process she had three new networking places to go where she was able to find many good prospects. As a result, her business skyrocketed.

If you are looking for a type of personality, then when you go to a networking event, find a person in that group with that personality and ask then where they congregate, what events they attend, charities they belong to, and associations they frequent. You will find that they tend to be involved with a lot of people with the same personality. Find a person with a great attitude or energy and follow that energy.

Just as we explained that in sales everybody isn't a great fit, the same is true for networking. You don't want to meet everyone in the world. You will be most successful if you set limits on how many people you want to meet at any given event as well as who you want to meet. It works best to set a goal of 3 to 5 new quality contacts at each event. A quality contact is not just someone who can fog a mirror and has a pulse. You want to pay attention to the behavior, attitude, and values of the people you meet. Your connections will be stronger with people with whom you most identify.

Make a list of 10 qualities of an ideal client or customer. Then, keep that in mind as you meet new people. It also helps you describe to your referral partner in more detail what you are looking for in a potential client or customer.

An easy formula to follow for networking success is Sarah's 3+3+3 Formula. You find three targeted networking events a week, find three people to have coffee, lunch, dinner or a midnight snack with and contact three people you've known previously to ask them to help you expand your business. If you are too busy for 3-3-3, try 2-2-2 or 1-1-1. It's all about consistency.

Sarah has had people come to her and say that they want to double their business and in six to twelve months doing a 3-3-3 have been able to double, triple, and quadruple their business. It's powerful so long as you are sure that your networking places are indeed targeted to places where your customers or power partners are found.

Before you even attend your networking event, you want to do some of the following:

- ✓ Research the attendees if they are listed online, especially if it is an Expo.
- ✓ Make a list of some questions so conversation comes easily.
- ✓ Look up past events to determine the proper attire.
- ✓ Make sure you have enough business cards. Keep your cards, as much as possible, in the same place so you are not searching everywhere for them once you are at the event.
- ✓ Make certain you know what you want to tell others about what you do.

Usually when attending networking events, there is a period for open networking. If open networking is not specifically stated, come early and network. Sarah and Linda both love advising their clients to think of themselves as a host on the planet. You come with the intention to make people feel as if they are coming to a party at your home. As you would be there early, stand at the door and greet them, have a great, big smile on your face, and introduce them to others you know, etc. We want to emphasize that getting to an event early makes a big difference in the results you produce. First of all, when you are at an event early, you simply meet more people and get to talk to more people. Also, you can scout out more of the crowd.

Another reason to arrive early is often you will find the event planners there. This gives you a great opportunity to talk with them about who you would like to meet and ask them to make introductions for you. This saves you time and works wonders.

Also, be prepared to stay later than the event end time. You may meet a valuable contact and want to continue your conversation.

Often, networkers have the opportunity to spend a short amount of time, usually 30-seconds, to tell the group what they do. This is referred to as either an infomercial, 30-second commercial, or an elevator pitch (this term developed because it is about the time it takes to ride an elevator up with somebody.)

The following is an example of a 30 second commercial:

My name is Cecilia Jones. My company is Beautiful Interiors. We work with mid-size homeowners who want peace of mind and the very best interiors. Typically my clients complain about their home feeling dated, that they are confused about what is the right style for them and where to start. Again, my name is Cecilia Jones of Beautiful Interiors.

Sometimes when you are at a networking and the format allows for you to speak a little longer. To extend your elevator pitch to 60 seconds, you can add some of the following:

- A great referral for me is...
- How your product or service is distinct from others. [However, never bad mouth your competition.]
- Who you want to be connected with.

Always stop at 60 seconds!

Here's a formula to help you create your 30 second commercial:

<company logo>

Creating your 30 Second Commercial (elevator speech, intro, etc.)

Introduction:
My name is _____ and my company is _____

Educate and inform your listener:
We work with (professionals, people, company executives, etc.)
_____
_____

Describe how you help them (find peace, make money, create websites, etc.) – continue from above "we work with" (description of people), "who want to (fill in how you help them)
_____
_____.

You can add the following if time allows: Typically my clients (the people you work with) share the following characteristics. Say things like "...complain about... Look for...want...etc – this is how we can help."
_____
_____.

Closing:
Again, my name is: _____ I'm with: _____

Be sure to:
- Breathe
- Smile
- Make eye contact
- Speak with an appropriate tone (not too loud, not too soft)
- Speak at an appropriate pace (not too fast, not too slow)
- Time your infomercial to exactly 30 seconds. Stop at 30 seconds!

Always stop at 30 seconds!

The following is an example of a 60 second commercial:

My name is Cecilia Jones. My company is Beautiful Interiors. We work with mid-size homeowners who want peace of mind and the very best interiors. Typically, my clients complain about their home feeling dated, that they are confused about what is the right style for them and where to start. Again, my name is Cecilia Jones of Beautiful Interiors.

A great referral for me is someone who is moving, who has recently moved into a new home or who wants to redecorate. What makes me different from others is my understanding of what clients want and providing comfortable spaces. I would like to be connected with builders, contractors, and home owners.

If you have 2-minutes, do the following:

- Describe what you are qualified to do (degrees, certificates, special training, etc.)
- Add a story about a success or tell about a testimonial you received
- Use a memory hook, which is a tag line or short sentence that makes your business more memorable.

Always stop at 2 minutes!

The following is an example of a 2 minute commercial:

My name is Cecilia Jones. My company is Beautiful Interiors. We work with mid-size home owners who want peace of mind and the very best interiors. Typically, my clients complain about their home feeling dated, that they are confused about what the right style is for them and where to start. Again, my name is Cecilia Jones of Beautiful Interiors.

A great referral for me is someone who is moving, who has recently moved into a new home or who wants to redecorate. What makes me different from others is my understanding of what clients want and providing comfortable spaces. I would to be connected with builders, contractors, and home owners.

I have special training from Paris. Recently I had a client tell me that by working with me, they came in under budget, under time, and over on results. When you want the very best, remember us at Beautiful Interiors.

Sometimes you don't even have 30 seconds to get your point across. Sarah was getting off of an airplane with a CEO of a major corporation. As they were exiting, he asked, "So what do you do, Sarah?"

Sarah realized that she didn't have 30 seconds. She'd be lucky to have 10. As they walked off the plane down the ramp, Sarah blurted out, "I work with CEO's and sales people who want to sell more and speakers who want to speak brilliantly."

The CEO stopped in his tracks and said, "I need you. Here's my card, give me a call."

If you need to tell someone in a very short time what you do, the following *Benefit Statement Formulas* will help you say what you do in ten seconds. This will help you say what you do so people want to buy from you.

We are(I am) best known for (result) _____.

We/I work with _____ who want _____.

My mission is to _____ for (particular group) _____.

Note: Try using visual imagery whenever possible as it is memorable. Avoid the use of the word 'you' in your benefit statement as it is too strong and comes off as too pushy in verbal interactions. Use only positives in benefit statements.

Qualify your target:

Once you're comfortable introducing yourself, you want to know what to say to both find your networking partners and know who you can help. We do this by asking the *Qualifying Question*. Think of something to ask that will generate a pain statement. Here are some examples:

Business Coach: How is your business? People will respond by telling what they see as a problem or they will tell you about everything that is going very well. Those who disclose a problem with you are your potential clients.

Heating and Air Conditioning Company: Have you checked your heating and air system lately? If someone has not done that in their home for a while, that may be a potential client.

Financial Advisor: Have you made a financial plan lately? If they haven't it's possible they may need your help.

By asking these questions, you can usually determine if you are talking to someone who you can possibly help.

Now, you can also determine that, in fact, at this time, he or she is just not a good fit for your business. In that case, that person may fall into one of the Referral Partner categories:

Basic Referral Partner

This is the lowest level of referral partner. If you have not been networking a long time and do not have a strong networking base, you may want to set an appointment to meet with this person. This is someone who likely just wants to meet with you to see if you can refer business to them and is anyone who could possibly introduce you to simply another basic referral partner. At this meeting, you will learn about that person and you both will have the opportunity to refer others. These may not be direct referrals that are possible customers or clients, but the people to whom they refer you may know some possible clients for you.

Strategic Partner

These relationships develop because both you and this other person may be able to offer something to the shared target audience that is appropriate for you both. As an example, you may want to work together to create a seminar, a workshop, a podcast, webinar, etc. Having discussions during the meetings that you set-up will help you make this kind of a determination.

Power Partner

This is a person whose business compliments yours. As an example, a furniture store and someone who delivers furniture, a fitness coach and nutritionist or chiropractor and a physical therapist. These are people who regularly give referrals back and forth to one another.

Center of Influence

a.   This is the highest level of Referral Partner. You invite this partner for a meeting, usually a coffee or meal.

You explain the requirements to become a Center of Influence partner, as follows:

Must have a broad network and be a person of influence
Have the capacity to help you
Want to help you
You must agree to give each other 2-3 referrals a year.

b.   Along with the benefit of getting 2-3 referrals a year, you both agree to stay in touch about once a month by giving one another suggestions such as a good business book, a great article, a new, exciting website, an important event, a new place to network, etc.

c.   If you enter into this arrangement, and one of you falls short of the commitment, then that person drops out of the relationship.

Referral Partner Meeting

Often when people get together to get to know one another so that they can help each other by making referrals, the meetings run on, fun is had by all, but most often substantive referrals do not happen. First, it is necessary, to have some time in the beginning of the meeting for rapport. It is during this time that you find commonalties and generally find ways to get to know or trust someone. However, to get the best results, use the following form, the Referral Profile. The example below is the one Linda used for her company when she was doing group coaching. The headings are there; just fill in your own information.

\<company logo\>

Perhaps these thoughts will be helpful when
you're talking with others

What to look for:

- Small business owners, solopreneurs, managers, and other professionals
- Working women and men who are unhappy with their current career
- Smart, savvy, educated professionals who don't believe they have accomplished what they believe they should, or have attained the success they believe they deserve
- Successful men and women, owners, and corporations that want help getting to the next level
- Successful business owners and professionals who want more, who want to better organize or monetize their businesses.

What to listen for:

- "I want to take my career or business to the next level."
- "I'm looking for some tools and tactics that will make a difference in my business, to make more money or get more clients"
- "I wish I were doing something else. I want help finding a way to have passion in my work and make money too"
- "I love what I do and I've had tremendous success, but I want more." Or, "I am working too hard and need processes and systems to have more balance in my life."
- "I am so close to achieving the goals I have been working on for so long; I think I need some outside help."

Ideal prospect description:

- A small business owner, solopreneur, manager, or other professional committed to the journey of self-improvement
- Professionals who seek to harness their personal power and achieve clarity of purpose

- Working men and women who seek a better balance between their work lives and their personal lives
- Business women and men who want powerful, measurable results
- A corporation that wants to help its employees achieve clarity, balance, power, and results

What to say to that prospect

- "I have the perfect company to help you. Can I give them your info and have them call you?"
- "[Your Business Name] works with professional men and women to help them go from where they are to where they want to be."
- "[Your Business Name] has a variety of programs to choose from to meet the individual needs of their clients."
- "[Your Business Name] more than 500 clients grow professionally since the year 2000."
- "[Your Business Name] is about action and with more than 6 decades of working with business owners and professionals has amassed the resources, solutions, tools, and tactics that really work."

Strategic Alliances

- Coaches, Bankers, Accountants, and Attorneys
- Marketing and IT firms
- Professional Associations
- Elevated Networkers
- Other Consultants

Thank you

If you are standing with a hot prospect or someone who is a strong referral partner, the easiest way to follow-up and get an appointment is to recommend setting an appointment on the spot. 99% of the time the other person will readily agree. You simply say, "Why don't we make an appointment to get together? I have my calendar right here."

It avoids the "I call you," "You call me," "I call your grandmother's best friends' brother" syndrome.

Some people may not be comfortable or able to set the appointment at that moment. Don't panic. Simply say, "I would love to meet with you. May I contact you?" Please tell them when you expect to contact them – and then do so!

We have seen countless people mess up their closing opportunities as a result of poor follow-through. We strongly believe that all interactions between networkers must be permission based. The reason for this is that it is simply courteous to determine first if someone wants to know who you are and what you do or if they want your business card. It is important to emphasize that if you either give your business card to someone who hasn't asked you for it or you start a dissertation on what you do before determining that the other person in interested, you will turn off that person. So be careful about this.

If you have opted for the second action above, to ask someone to contact them, not only will it hurt your business not to follow-up, it is discourteous. Therefore, you must have a CRM (Customer Relationship Management) system. This simply is a way to keep a record of the person's contact information, where you met the person, when you met the person, something such as the way he or she looked, what they wore or what they said so you keep track appropriately. Contact that person by email or phone and follow-through to set the appointment.

Another reason it is important to have a CRM is that – as much as we would love otherwise – a sale does not always materialize. That doesn't mean you can't keep a relationship going. We never know when someone develops a need for what we offer or has someone to refer to us.

It's a good idea to have some kind of a Tickler system. That is way of saying that we are tickling ourselves to remember. If someone seems very important to you either as a potential client or a referral partner, use the following as a guide:

Contact them within 3 days of meeting them, preferably with a hand-written note (if they are really a VIP) followed by a phone call or email.

3 weeks later contact them again and every 3 months after that. Be creative with your reasons for contacting them such as sending them an interesting article, or letting them know about an event coming up, or interviewing them for an article you are writing so that you don't just say "Hi, I want your business."

However, there are different degrees of importance in networking relationships. There may some people that your sense tells you don't need to contact every 3 months. In that case, you may to choose twice a year or annually.

Getting back to the event, there are a few major concerns some of our clients have had. The number one question we get is "What do I say?" Here are a few answers to get you started:

- What brings you to this event?
- What do you do?
- What's most important to you? (Answers may say, "my business, my family, my sport activity, etc.)
- Are you a member of this organization? Or, How long have you been a member of this organization.
- What's next for you?

Another question we get frequently is "How do I get away from someone who's talking my ear off?" A good reply is to thank him or her for their time and information. Then, say, "I'm sure you want to network so I'll let you meet some more people." Another way to do this is to find someone in the crowd you can go over to talk with, say to the person who is going on and on, "Oh, there's Mary [or whatever name of the person you do actually see.] I better go over and talk to her. It's been wonderful chatting with you. I hope you enjoy the rest of the event." Then, make a bee line for Mary.

Quite often, people ask us, "How do I remember names?" There are several techniques you can use.

One is the *kinesthetic technique*, which is when you write the person's name with your finger in the air. They'll never notice and it works.

The second one is the *three times technique* when you get their name into the conversation three times while you are speaking to them. For example, "Hi Tom, it's great to meet you. So, Tom, "Tell me what you do." And a little later, say, "It was great to meet you Tom.

The last one is the *Smash Technique*, which is when you take their name and you match it with something similar. Then, you smash the two images – their name and something that is dramatic, funny, or interesting. For example, if the name is Jennifer Tomkins, you might think "Pumpkin" and imagine the pumpkin smashing into Jennifer.

Return on Investment

Many people ask how they evaluate the value of their networking groups. In the context of choosing a place to network, much time and money gets invested in a group. What kind of formal measurements can we perform to determine whether or not our time and money will come back to us in bonafide leads for business?

Let's say a group costs $360 to join for the year. Now, if you spend one meeting a month in this group, and a meeting lasts two hours, you add to the cost of dues the cost of your time, in this case about 24 hours for the year. Do you know what your time is worth?

As it relates to total investment, if your time is worth $100 an hour then your total annual investment in this example group is $2400 in time and another $360 in dues for a total investment of $2760. Is this amount too high? That all depends on your return against this investment.

If your average sale is $5,000, then even with one piece of new business, your return on your investment is pretty good. However, if your average sale is $100, you need to close 28 new orders to break even on your investment in the group.

In the diagram below, choose one of the three groups that you identified as a good fit with your target market. Determine your total investment in terms of time and money in this group. Now that you know what you are investing in time and money through your participation, you want to further figure out how much new business you have to close to make this investment pay off.

Now let's document of the other part of the equation: how many new orders must you close to make your investment pay off?

Divide the total investment by the average revenue of a closed piece of business. How many orders do you need to break even? Is this volume reasonable? Is it achievable? If you answer yes to these questions then this group is a good fit based on the strategy of return on investment. If the answers are "no," then maybe this group isn't a good fit.

Return on Investment - *Example...*

Financial investment:	Dues of $360	$360
Time investment:	24 hours at $100/hr	$2,400
Total investment:	$360 + $2,400 =	$2,760
Sales:	1 average sale of $5,000	$5,000
RETURN:	$5,000 - $2,770 =	$2,230

For this group...

Financial investment:		
Time investment:		
Total investment:		

Sales needed:	Total investment divided by average sale =	

A third strategic measure for choosing a network group can be how well we feel aligned with the group in terms of our values and ethics. If one of your values is actually the attainment of business and the value emphasized by the group you may be checking out is more about social relationships, you may not be a good fit.

Perhaps one group requires its members to generate a specific number of leads. That might create an ethical dilemma if you feel compelled to offer low quality leads just to satisfy that requirement.

Alignment with Values and Ethics

Your values/ethics:	Group's values/ethics:
•	•
•	•
•	•

Chapter Seven

Sensational Sales Scripts

Many people are uncomfortable with what is often a common perception of sales. What may come to mind is the sleazy, pushy salesperson that uses manipulation and tricks to force someone into buying something.

Good selling is the complete opposite. It's helping people make a decision to get something that truly benefits them.

For many people there are a lot of scary parts of selling. Often one of the scariest parts for the business person has to do with sales scripts. That is because frequently people are concerned that a formal script will make them sound phony, they'll have trouble remembering what they are supposed to say, and that they will be focusing more on trying to say exactly what is in the script rather than what they really want to convey.

Once you get used to them, a sales script is an effective tool. Some people are more comfortable with a bullet point outline and others a written sales script. However, it allows you to include all the concepts of good selling and actually helps you cover all the important points.

There are several times when you need a sales script. We believe the ones that will be most important to you are: when setting a phone appointment, when doing a live appointment and when closing the sale.

In a phone appointment, you want to do the following:

- ✓ Remind the person where you met them and the conversation you had
- ✓ Determine if the person is able to talk at this time.
- ✓ Build rapport

✓ Establish the purpose of the call
✓ Get them talking about their pain or gain
✓ Agree to meet in person and set up details about the appointment.

Example:

Hello John:

This is Mary Jones. We met at the Grandville Chamber last Friday and talked a little about the challenges you were having in your business. (phone system, marketing, etc.)

Am I calling a good time? (If not, thank them for their time and arrange a convenient time for both of you for the next call.)

Tom was sure a great speaker, don't you think? I know how much you love the chamber. I thought it was a really nice event.

The purpose for my call today is to talk with you a little about a possible solution for the challenges you were having in your business. What is the biggest challenge for you? (Or gain: What would be the best thing that could happen a year from now?)

Would you like some help with that? Great, how about [arrange date, time, place, etc.?]

In an in-person meeting, you want to include:

✓ Reminder of the phone conversation.
✓ Permission for time frame
✓ Outline the meeting format
✓ Get more detailed information about the person with whom you are meeting. Ask a lot of questions.
✓ Explore their challenges, problems, and desires. Ask a lot of questions.
✓ Ask if they are interested in getting help for what they have told you.
✓ Ask if they would like your help.

Example:

Stacy, on the phone, we talked about your challenges with [repeat challenges from phone conversation.]
We agreed to meet from 9 a.m. to 10:00 a.m., is that right?
What we are going to do is talk in a little more detail about you and your business [phone system, marketing, etc.], then we are going to delve a bit more into your issues and goals, and see if we agree that we are a good fit for one another. Does that sound good to you?
So tell me, Stacy, how long have you had this situation? [Get this person to share as much information as possible.]
Do you want help with that?
[If yes] I think I can help you with that.
[If no, go over the challenges and issues again.] You didn't want any help on that?
This will illicit some concerns such as cost or time commitment. Address those concerns.

We mentioned a closing script. Actually, our closing took place at the end of our in-person meeting. When you close, be sure to nail down certain details. By that we mean, emphasize some of the conversation about the pain or gain. Once you have a sense that your prospect feels the need to get help, that's when you offer your help, which is the solution to the pain or for the gain.

Below are some common objections to overcome and some ideas on how to respond during the close:

- I don't have the money – If money were no object, would there be any other reason you wouldn't want to do this [or purchase this] right now? *This will often uncover the real reason.*
- It's too expensive – I understand how you feel. I know a lot of people who feel the same way, and what they found is it's actually very reasonable

when you amortize it over twelve months. [Or, …
when you think about how healthy you will feel;
or when you think about how much it's going to
save you in the long run.]

- I don't have the time – How much time are you
thinking it's going to take? [Usually, your prospect
is thinking it is going to take way longer than it
actually will.]

- I already have one – Are you happy with the one
you have now?

- It's not the right time – What would have to
happen to make it the right time?

The main point to keep in mind when creating or using
a script is that you want to respond most often with a
question rather than a defensive comment.

Remember that practice will help you get used to using
sales scripts. When you use them over and over your will
realize how much benefit they are to you.

Great Sales Presentations:

Linda had an opportunity to get one of her biggest new
clients in her former business. She worked so hard and
prepared for a long time on what she thought was a
beautiful presentation filled with diagrams, pie charts,
pictures of her beautiful trucks, and hundreds of pages of
text. As she sat at the table with the President and five
other executives of this company, she was about half-way
through, when she noticed the president had been resting
his head in his hand and his head slipped off his hand
because he was nodding off. She saw that he looked
incredibly bored. She nevertheless kept on with her
presentation. Although she was very uncertain about how
to respond, she blurted out, "What do you want?"

He then began listing several points that were
important to him and everything changed in the

appointment. That was a very good lesson because from then on, Linda realized that she needed to focus on asking questions and listening carefully rather than going on and on about the great beauty of her presentation.

As in all sales situations, ask questions at the beginning of your presentation. Sometimes questions are not allowed at which point you want to start with something that will grab attention.

Five Secrets to a Great Sales Presentation

Secret #1 – Use Power Point Effectively - If you have the opportunity to use Power Point or another similar program be sure and use fewer than three lines on a slide and use photos that create emotions on as many slides as possible. Remember to continue facing the audience and not have your head turned away to the screen.

Secret #2 – Using the screen to your advantage – Always try to put the screen or screens, not directly behind you, but to your left or right. Then you're free to stand in the power position of center stage.

Secret #3 – Kill the podium – try never to stand behind the podium. It is a giant block between you and the audience you would like want to connect with. See if you can have it moved to the side or even removed. If you need notes, either put them on the podium to the side of you or get a small low table to put them on. It is preferable to not have notes at all or spend as little time as possible staring down at your notes.

Secret #4 – 3 Questions Technique – One of the best ways to engage your audience in a presentation is to ask three relevant questions. Sarah worked with a manufacturing company that gives sales presentations to Coke, Pepsi and Quaker as well as other Fortune 500 companies. They originally did Sales Presentations that started with fifteen minutes about how great their company was. Sarah had to reverse the order of the slide in the Power Point so that the section about their company was both reduced and put at the end.

Now to the opening of this company's sales presentation...they begin with three relevant questions to the audience asking the following:

1. What projects are you currently working on?
2. What challenges do they create for you?
3. What projects to you see coming in the future?

There closing rate doubled almost instantly! Try to ask three similar, relevant questions at the beginning of the presentation that you know your audience will be happy to answer. Avoid saying, "Hi, it's nice to be here," or "Thank you for having us" or any fluff that does not move your cause forward. These kinds of fillers only slow down the reaction you want from your presentation.

Secret #5 – Get into the mind of your prospect – It's more important to put yourself in the shoes of your prospect than to have flashy displays, forty page brochures or power points with nine rows of texts.

Sarah once worked with an organization that was trying to get a million dollar grant. The people in charge of the grant had narrowed it down to the final three and had fifty people from the organization coming to watch the three non-profits do their presentations about why they should get the million dollar grant.

The Non-profit Sarah was working with was the tiniest and the least known of the three and least likely to get the grant. Sarah took a look at their presentation and was shocked to discover the driest most cerebral pitch she had ever seen. It included nine lines of text on almost every slide and charts and graphs that were unintelligible.

Sarah told them to imagine themselves as the audience watching this presentation and they began to change everything. Photos and videos that were emotionally stirring were added and almost everything else was taken out. The presenters told story after story of the compelling results they created at their non-profit. At the end of the evening at the presentation, the organization Sarah was working with was awarded the million dollar prize!

Similarly, Linda recalls when sales people would come to her company and do their sales presentations. They came armed with brochures, charts, graphs and other boring collateral materials. She truly felt repelled by these approaches. It was clear that these presenters felt that their company was so great that she had no choice but to choose their company. However, Linda felt that they really didn't care about her company needs. Rather, she felt that they ignored what she cared about and wanted only to impress her.

In one-on-one presentations come armed with questions because the quality of your life will be determined by the quality of your questions. Some of these questions might be:

"What is important to you right now at your company?"
"What makes that so important?"
"What's going well?"
"What concerns do you have?"
"What are your top frustrations and challenges"

Always remember that you are in front of your prospect to help them. If you focus on getting in their mind so you determine what they want, rather than trying to impress them, you will have much greater success.

Section Three
Speaking

Chapter Eight

How to Speak Brilliantly

There are many reasons why speaking can help your career or your company. You can use speaking to move up the corporate ladder, to speak your way to more business, to show off your company, your product, or your service, to pitch for funding, and to gain exposure and credibility or even go on to be a professional speaker.

Sarah has spoken nationally and internationally to over 1000 prestigious organizations and Linda has spoken to hundreds as well. As a result of this experience, we have learned some secrets that we are going to share with you about how to use speaking to build your business, build your sales, and your overall success.

The number one reason that people don't take advantage of this incredible tool of public speaking is fear! Speaking is the number one fear in America followed by death which is number two. Number three is death while public speaking... just kidding! People would rather die than speak in public. We'd rather be in the box than giving a eulogy.

Here are five tactics for overcoming fear when you do public speaking:

1.   Have a mission when you speak that is stronger than your fear. An example could be, "I want to help my audience grow and succeed." When your mission is stronger than your fear, you can do anything.

2.   Visualize the speaking engagement or sales presentation going exceedingly well.

3.   Take a deep breath, even if you have to go to the restroom for some quiet time. One exercise actors use is the panting dog technique. You pant breath from your belly a few times until your body begins to relax.

4.   Another technique is use the tense and release method. When you are nervous before your speech, take a deep breath in and tense every muscle in your body including your face. Breathe out and release all the tension and the fear.

5.   Power poses can be your best friend. Studies show that standing in superman poses can give you instant confidence. Stand with your arms on your hips, looking up, shoulders back, and take a big power breath. Hold it for, at least, thirty seconds.

If you want to speak brilliantly, there is one thing you must do that will make you 75% better as a speaker, instantly. The best speakers you've ever seen are doing this either consciously or unconsciously. Your secret weapon is called A Super Objective.

Super Objective

A Super Objective is your overall goal, vision, or dream for your speech. It is the ultimate, best thing that could happen as a result of your speech for the audience.

It is a mantra you can say to yourself right before you go on stage that will center you, give you confidence, and a sense of purpose.

A Super Objective is a short statement that often includes what you want the audience to feel and how you would like them to change by the end of the speech. It's much like a bull's-eye and your message, the arrow, headed toward that bull's-eye.

An example of a Super Objective is "I want people to be inspired and to grow." Simple, short, and easy to remember, but something you're passionate about. Super Objectives include your values and sense of purpose.

This is not the same as your personal goals, though personal goals are very important too. Your personal goals might look like, "I want people to buy from me, ""I want people to be impressed with my company" or "I want them to like me." Personal goals are important to recognize within you, but a Super Objective is in the highest and best interest of the audience only.

Sarah has seen speakers she has coached go from mediocre to megastar by having a powerful Super Objective.

The Five Part Magic Formula for Making a Great Speech

When you need to put together a great speech, here are five easy things you can do to put one together relatively quickly:

1. Your first action is to make a list of absolutely everything that you would want into your speech that fits with your Super Objective.

2. Create a list of stories you like to tell or you think are applicable. One way to create great stories is to look at the significant events in your life and make a list of them, starting from when you were very young up until now. List the things have happened to you that you would consider significant. Don't worry, at this stage, about what points the story would make, just make the list first. Then, look at all of your significant life events and see if any of them make points that would fit with your Super Objective and the points within your speech. Be sure to

include what Sarah calls drop-in stories. Drop-in stories have four parts in a speech.

Part One – A client had a problem or a desire
Part Two – What I or my company did about it
Part Three – The incredible results
Part Four – How this applies to the audience

If you want to sell your product, your services or your company, drop-ins will do it gracefully without your having to even push or seem sales-y.

3. Use the Storyboard Technique. That's where you put all the pieces that you want to fit in your speech on old-fashioned index cards. Of course, some people do that on their Power Point. But, index cards allow you to move all the pieces around on the table or bulletin board so you can see how to possibly structure your speech visually.

Sarah felt fortunate to have learned this observing the writers at Disney doing storyboards for their movies. They would have cartoons drawn of all the different scenes and have them on bulletin boards. They would say things like, "What if we put the end at the beginning?" or "What if we put the beginning at the end?" or "What if we moved the scenes around in the middle?" This allowed them to create the best possible story line for the film.

4. Icons – You can use drawings, clip art, or symbols for each piece of your speech on each index card as it is easier to retain a picture than it is to retain a bunch of words. For example, one card might be a story about a house. Why not just draw a house on the index card? Another index card might be your introduction with questions of the audience. Why not just have questions marks? Ultimately you can take all of these icons and pictures, and put them on one single sheet and be able to know your whole speech without reading it. On the back of each

index card, you can put all the bullet points that you want to make sure you remember in that section of the speech. Then, memorizing all the points of your speech becomes very easy. You use your index cards like third graders use flash cards to learn 3x3=9. Quiz yourself on each card while you're standing in line at Starbucks or sitting in traffic.

5. The Fifteen-Minute Maximum Technique – When you practice your speech do not memorize the whole entire thing. It will make you crazy. You may want to memorize the first couple of lines of your opening or close, but aside from that, use bullet points to jump off and make it sound fresh every time. Unless you are a trained actor do not memorize every line.

The Fifteen-Minute Maximum comes in when you start practicing your speech. Practice the most difficult parts of your speech in 15-minute maximums. This avoids burn out and creates a greater likelihood that you will practice because it is not an overwhelming amount of time. For example, let's say you have a speech in three weeks. Schedule 15-minute rehearsals every day for three weeks. Do not do the whole, entire speech in that 15-minute segment. Break it down into chunks and work on different parts of the speech in different rehearsals.

This is how Sarah used to direct plays. You wouldn't rehearse the entire play from beginning to end over and over and over again. You'd chunk down the scenes, and spend more time on the more difficult scenes and less time on the easier ones. For most people the opening is the most difficult scene. Spend a lot more time rehearsing the opening than anything else.

The other thing that people tend to forget to work on is the close because they usually will rehearse from beginning to end, beginning to end, beginning to end without ever actually getting to the end.

If you are ever at a loss for how to structure a speech, open with three questions for the audience, make a point, tell a story, doing something interactive, and then repeat make a point, tell a story, doing something interactive until it's time to close the speech. Close with a call to action for the audience.

An interactive is anything when you get an audience to raise a hand, turn to a partner and discuss, write something down, or shout out an answer. The reason an interactive every 5 to 7 minutes is so important is that we are used to watching television, where there is a break about every 7 minutes. So, make sure you change course in some way about every 7 minutes.

A Call to Action is where you sum up everything you've said in such a way that you can tell the audience where you want them to go and what you want them to do with all the information you've shared.

One example is "Choose one thing from all we've talked about today that you are really going to take action on. Who here can think of one thing they could really do starting right away? Because I believe in you and I believe you deserve to double your business, double your impact and change the world."

Chapter 9

Open with Strength

There are six essentials for success in your opening.

ONE

Show your credibility. One way to make sure you have credibility is to have a written introduction so an Introducer can introduce you powerfully. Rather than just hand them your biography, which is not necessarily meant to be read aloud, use the 3-part formula for a great introduction (see example below.)

   a. Topic
   b. Importance
   c. Person

Topic - When writing your introduction start with the topic you will speaking about as that is usually more compelling than talking about you first.

Importance - Then, move on to the importance of the topic to the audience.

Person - Finally, talk about you the person and all of your many accolades as they relate to the topic.

An example of a professional introduction would be, "Today our topic is the Power of Leadership." As business leaders and managers, we all want to become the best leaders we can possibly be. We are very fortunate to have Joan Smith as our speaker as she has the perfect background to share with us the secrets of great leadership. Joan is CEO of ABC Company, is President of the Phoenix Chamber of Commerce, and has a MBA from Northwestern University. She's spoken for The Professional Managers Association, IBM, and Farmers Insurance. Her book, *The Power of Leadership*, is a best seller. Please give a warm welcome to Joan Smith.

You may also want to tell a story about your background in the beginning of your speech that leads people to your credibility. Your story can be done in a Leader's Legacy format. There are ten steps to constructing a great Leader's Legacy story.

Step One: Set the Stage – For example, "It was 1990 and I was on the phone with my mom when she said, "You're a great teacher, but you really should be in sales or leadership. It would be great if you could work with Dad in the business. So I talked to my Dad and he said, 'What the heck do you know about the scrap metal business?' I said, "I don't, but I'll learn!'"

Step Two: Paint the picture of the dream – For example, "I dreamed of big sales and our business becoming a multi-million dollar business employing dozens of people."

Step Three: The Big Challenges – For example, "But things were tough; competition was fierce, the industry people weren't thrilled to see a woman show up, and it was a recession. When I went into factories hoping to get business, owners of companies would have their feet up on their desks because there wasn't any business to be had."

Step Four: Absolute Low Point – For example, "It was Christmas eve, snowy and freezing cold. I walked into my dingy office, sat at my desk, put my head down and cried."

Step Five: The Realization – For example, "I realized at that moment that everything had to change."

Step Six: The Grand Motivation – For example, "I read every book I could get my hands on, I spoke to everybody who would listen, I became a sponge in learning everything I could about leadership and sales."

Step Seven: The Climb Up – For example, "The next thing I knew I got a phone call and it was Whirlpool. They want to do a lot of business with us. Next, we hired an Operations Manager, and with my father ill and finally passing away, I took over. We got a new building, sales were way up, and we hired more people."

Step Eight: The High Point – For example, "Finally we grew beyond even my wildest dreams to well over six million in sales."

Step Nine: The Call to Help Others – For example, " People started asking me how did you do all that you have done in sales and as a leader and that's when I found my calling to help other people become successful as well."

Step Ten: The Tie-in to the Speech – For example, "Today I am going to share with you 7 secrets you can use to be more successful in your business and personal life, things I learned from my own experiences and from the hundreds of clients I have supported in finding their dreams."

Leaders Legacy

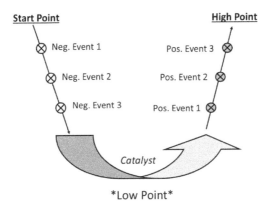

Low Point

TWO

Show Your Care, Find a way to let the audience know that you care about the audience's needs, wants, and desires. One way to do that is to start your program with questions to the audience. Such as:

a. Who here would like to double their business in the next year?
b. Who would like double the impact they have on everyone around them?
c. Would anyone like to change the world a little bit for the better?

Or, another example would be "Who can tell me how many snack foods Americans consume every day? What snack foods do they consume most? And, what's your favorite snack food?

Or, "How many people would like to have their Elevator Pitch be a little bit better? In one or two words, how would you liked to be perceived after your elevator pitch? So, if we could do magic, what would you have liked to have learned by the end of our time together today?

THREE

Show You Have a Mission. Share your Super Objective or purpose for the speech with the audience so they know where you are going.

FOUR

Share What's In It For the Audience – For example, you might say, "Today you will discover all the secrets you need to know to be able to formulate your product faster and while saving money."

FIVE

Use Your Core Competencies – Do what you are best at first in your speech. If you are a great story teller, start with a story. If you are good at asking questions, start with questions. Do you love quotes, start with a quote.

SIX

Get them on the Train – Imagine someone says to you, "Get on the train, we're leaving and we'll be gone for an hour with no explanation of why you should get on a train. That is exactly what you are asking an audience to do. If you were to say "We're going to have great food and see waterfalls and there'll be guys in togas and girls in bikinis and in the end there will be fireworks" you'd be more likely to get on the train. Always remember you have to get them on the train and that at every transition they have the opportunity to get back off if you don't keep selling them on what comes next.

Stories and Examples Sell It Best – People always tell Sarah, "I know I should have stories in my speaking but where shall I find them?" to which she replies, "Stories are everywhere and examples plentiful if you just look."

When looking for personal stories, start with your own life history. What events have been significant to you? Start with a history of your life. Ask yourself what was it, when was it, and what made it significant? Not all of your stories will be gems, but one or two is all you need. Look through your whole life for significant events. They can be small things or big things: death of a parent or a first toy.

Well known speaker and author, Ian Percy, tells a story that makes a wonderful point, but isn't about anything spectacular. In his story, he says, "One day I ran out of tooth paste so I tossed out the tube. The next day I forgot to buy tooth paste so I pulled the tooth paste out of the trash, dusted off a couple of hairs, and used the tooth paste again. The next day I forgot again. Now, I'm taking a comb and squeezing the tooth paste out. The day after that I was mashing the tooth brush into the tooth paste and that's when I realized we are just like a tube of tooth paste. Just when we think we haven't got a single thing left, there's always more we have to give."

Chapter Ten

How to Choose the Right Speaking Topic for You

Many of our clients come to us knowing that they would like to speak and that it would be a big boon to their business, but not knowing what to speak about. There are four compelling factors to consider when choosing a topic: passion, expertise, desires of the meeting planners or program chair [person who hires the speaker], and the true needs of the audience.

Passion
You must speak about something you care about. Otherwise, the speech will be flat. If you must speak about something you are not particularly passionate about find an underlying truth you can tie to the speech to make it more compelling. For example, you can even speak on Underwater Basket Weaving providing you had a passion for helping people learn new things.

Let's say you have to speak about a very dry financial topic...but you have a passion for personal growth. The important point here is to tie personal growth to your financial topic.

Expertise
Speak about something that you know backwards and forwards. Do not speak on topics you don't know anything about and have to research! The other thing that people do is undervalue their own expertise because they think that everybody already knows what they know, and nothing could be further from the truth.

Linda truly identifies with this novice error. She was convinced that in order to be interesting and demonstrate expertise that she had to research and construct speeches that were, in her mind, more authoritative than her way of expressing her ideas. It took some considerable flops for her to realize that what people really wanted was her genuine expertise.

People will come to Sarah and say, "I have thirty years of experience in this and I know everything there is to know about this topic, but why would anyone want to hear this from me?"

Sarah tells them that everybody underestimates how interesting and valuable their life experience is. Because to them it *is just their life!* To illustrate this point, she tells them about Jeff Salz. When she first met Jeff, he was an up-and-coming speaker and author.

One day over lunch, she casually asked, "How did you become an anthropologist and adventurer?"

And, he told her about his friend Steve McAndrews. When Jeff was in high school, Steve moved to New Jersey from Texas. Steve was a tall, good-looking guy and Jeff was a short, chubby guy, whose nickname was "puffy".

One day Steve came to Jeff and said, in his Texas accent, "Je-iff, we have to go to Patagonia and climb a mountain because life is an adventure. Jeff said, "It sounds cold."

Steve said, "Je-iff if we go to Patagonia and climb a mountain that no one has ever climbed before, we can name the mountain."

Jeff said, "No thanks!"

Steve said, "But, Je-iff if we climb the mountain and name the mountain, when we come back girls will like you!" Jeff started packing.

Jeff and Steve went to Patagonia and started climbing the mountain. They had two people with them. At night, Jeff slept on an ice face slightly above where Steve was. In the morning, Jeff came down to find his best friend and

Steve wasn't moving. Jeff said, "Come on get up; it's not funny." And, much to his horror discovered that Steve was dead. Jeff was devastated.

Jeff decided to dedicate his life to living the adventures that Steve would never have. He floated around Lake Titicaca, he climbed many mountains, he met Aborigines, and finally, even decided to go back and climb the mountain that had killed his friend.

When he reached the top, he named the mountain Mount McAndrews and read a letter to his friend that he spiked into the ground at the top of the mountain. The letter read, "This is for you, Steve. You've made my life an adventure."

Sarah looked across the table at Jeff, with tears in her eyes and said, "So, Jeff, do you tell that story in your speeches?"

Jeff replied, "No, who'd be interested in that?"

Sarah told him "everyone!"

Years later Jeff is still telling the story. He has become one of the top speakers in the world and has even been inducted into the Speakers Hall of Fame.

So you have more interesting content and stories in you than you even realize.

How do I know what to put in my speech? – Stories.

If you find yourself telling the same story frequently over a beer, and people laugh or people cry or people ask you to tell the story again, you probably have a story that's worth putting in a speech as long as there is a way to tie that story to your topic.

For example, if you're speaking about sales and you have a story about running a marathon that story may tie into the point of determination in your speech.

How do I know what to put in my speech? – Content

If you find yourself giving the same advice over and over and over again or making the same points to a client those are things to capture for your speech.

What not to put in your speech.

You don't have room in your speech for every story. So choose the best stories you possibly can. Never do a story that is offensive to women, to a particular religion or race or political party. Never tell a story that is sexual, scatological, or scandalous. Never tell a story that is going to hurt anybody. Never tell a story that may be harmful to you. Never tell a story that's boring. If you aren't certain about those judgments, get professional outside help.

Chapter Eleven

Insider Speaking Secrets

Use the space wisely

It's important to use your space or stage for maximum impact. diagram 11.1 on the following page represents the space or stage you will be using. The audience would be in front of 7, 8 and 9.

The most powerful place to be is number 5. For a tiny group, it would be number 8. So then, you might think, "Why don't I stand in 5 or 8 for the whole presentation if that's the most powerful spot?" Because it's boring! Try to use a little bit more of the space if you can.

The second most powerful spot in the space is number 4 or in a smaller audience, number 7. The next most powerful space would be number 6 and number 9. The weakest place is number 1 and number 3. Always look at the space from the audience's point of view to be sure you can be seen from every angle in the audience. For example, if there is a giant post in the middle of the audience, you may need to change where you stand to be seen.

Always come into the space from the left side of the space as since we read from left to right, people have a more positive response to you if you come into the space from the left side.

Connect with the audience

Just as your stage or space had nine squares so does your audience. Imagine your audience in nine squares as shown in diagram 11.2. If you're standing on the stage or space facing out to the audience, number 1, 2 and 3 would be closest to you. Most people have a tendency to just talk to the people in number 1, 2 and 3. Worse yet, they gaze over the heads of everyone without making eye contact with anyone in any of the squares at all.

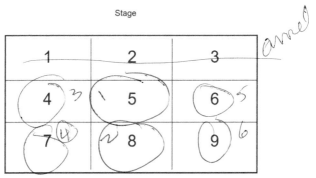

Diagram 11.1

Your job if you want to engage your audience is to talk to someone in each and every square. Obviously, you move your eye contact to another person every time you change gears in your thoughts. This strategy works with small groups all the way up to thousands.

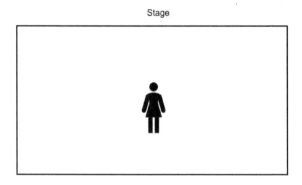

Diagram 11.2

The Desires of the Meeting Planners

You'll never speak either for pro bono or paid speaking if you can't tie your speech to the desires of the meeting planners. One way to find out their desires is to ask them, "what topics are you looking for, what topics have been popular in the past?" The other thing you can do is go online and read all the topics they've had in the recent past. A common mistake that many people make is to come up with a topic that no one is interested in seeing, when they could have easily translated their topic into something everyone would want.

Sarah had a client who came to her and said that he wanted to start speaking professionally. This man was a respected leader. However, he said that he intended to speak about solar eclipses. Sarah looked at him and said, "No. You speak on leadership and I will allow you one story about your adventures seeing a solar eclipse as long as you tie it back into leadership."

Pick a Topic People Actually Want to Hear

Sometimes speakers try to sell event planners and audiences on topics that they know would be valuable to them. But if the audience doesn't want these things, they will likely reject the topic. What the audience truly *wants* are all of the ideas, processes, systems, and content that they desire; however, they may not always know what they *need*. There is a distinction between what your audience likely needs and how you sell to them. When we use the term here "sell to them" we are referring to the marketing done ahead of your speech to get that speech accepted.

One example might be if we want to deliver content on the importance of a great mindset and all the strategies to have a better mindset, we would include these in our speech, but we would not use it sell to the audience in our marketing materials. Instead of talking about a great mindset, which might not be a popular topic, tie a great mindset into a topic such as Sales and Leadership, which is always popular. A speaker must discover how to market a topic so that the event planner and the audience feel compelled to hear that topic.

Never sell the true needs of the audience in your marketing to that audience; only sell them what they already want. A good example of this is when Linda saw a speaker whose topic was "Great Apps." Linda was prepared to take out a pillow and take a nap. She was shocked to discover the topic was fascinating because what it was really about was how to be better organized, more effective and more productive in your business.

If that speaker had simply titled his speech, "How to Be Better Organized, More Effective and More Productive in Your Business," Linda's attitude would have been completely different. The turn-out would have been different too. Rather, sell the *benefit*s to the audience. Sell your passion and sell the desires of the audience and the benefits of the speech, but never sell what only you believe the audience needs.

Where to Speak

The three goals you may likely have in speaking: you want to get paid to speak, you want to speak to get business or simply want to help the world. Those goals will influence where you choose to speak.

If you want to get paid to speak, there are many organizations that put requests for proposals right up on their website. For instance, when Linda transitioned from having owned her company to becoming a coach and speaker, she looked online to find organizations with local business owners that bring in speakers.

If you want to speak to get business, you must consider where your market congregates and speak there. Look up ten organizations in your local area that hire speakers similar to you, go to an event and listen to the speaker. Then, find a top-ranking member of the organization and say, "This is a wonderful organization. I can't believe I've never spoken here before."

They will reply, "Oh, you're a speaker?

You say, "Yes," and tell them your great topic. The top-ranking member will bring you over to the Program Chairs/Meeting Planners and introduce you as their new favorite speaker. The Program Chair, 80% of the time, will say, "Would you be interested in speaking to our organization? "

You reply, "Well, of course, I would love to speak here." The organization often plans their meetings months in advance so they may plug you in three or four months later.

Make sure you are dressed your best, you exude confidence, and of course, you have a great topic title.

If you simply want to help the world, you will want to find where the people are who need your message. However, Linda and Sarah feel that combining this with getting paid is even better. Our experience has shown that a client, an audience, a reader always feels a little better about paying some fee because they represent that with receiving value. Even charities may decide to cover your expenses and make a donation to their charity in your name.

Titles That Sell

One of the most important things that you need to do as a speaker is come up with an exceptional title for your speech. This will determine whether people will come out to hear you speak, whether you will be hired to speak, and how well the speech will be received.

Professional speakers live and die by how good their title is. Unless you are Oprah and people will come out to hear you no matter what, you need a great title for your speech.

Here's how you create a great title for your speech.

Step One: Start with a pool of words and phrases that are the benefits of your speech. For instance, your phrase pool might include "sell more" "success" "more profit."

In order to add to your phrase pool, here are three suggestions that will help a lot:

1. Ask friends and family for three words that describe you or the benefits of working with you.

2. Make a list of the benefits to the audience of your speech.

3. Make a list of 25 of your favorite words.

This makes an excellent phrase pool.

Step Two: Find thirty book titles that you love. Not books you love, but book *titles* that you love. You can do this by going to Amazon, a book store, library, or your own book shelf. You're looking for non-fiction titles, not *War and Peace or Tess of the D'Urbervilles.*

Step Three: Combine your word and phrase pool with your book titles to create new titles that sizzle and sell.

For example, if one of your titles is *Personal Power* by Tony Robbins and one of the words in your phrase pool is "sales" try "Sales Power." Now you have a fresh new title that you know will sell. Use this technique to come up with titles, sub-titles, section titles and copywriting for the description of the speech. If all else fails, title the speech "How to [do something] So You Can [get something else."] or, "7 Secrets to [the benefit of your speech.]"

20 Questions to Ask Meeting Planners

1. How long will I be speaking?

2. How many people are you anticipating?

3. Where's the event being held?

4. May I have a cell phone number in case I need to get a hold of you?

5. Would someone be able to print the handouts for the program or do I need to do that?

6. Is there anything else I can do to help you build excitement for the program or expand attendance for this event?

7. What is the main goal or purpose of the meeting? Does it have a special theme or name?

8. What is the ratio of males to females in the room?

9. May I have a list of attendees in advance and the companies or organizations they are with so I can customize my program for you?

10. How is the room set up?

11. What is the appropriate form of clothing to wear, formal, semi-formal, business, business casual, etc.

12. Will the eating portion be done by the time I start speaking?

13. If you have a microphone, may I have a cordless lavaliere microphone?

14. Does your group have any likes or dislikes from their speakers? Are there any topics that should be avoided or are sensitive to the group right now?

15. Who will be introducing me? (Then, of course, send that person your introduction.)

16. What time do the first people arrive at the event? (You want to arrive at the time that the first people arrive.)

17. Would you please forward any promotion materials you use for this program?

18. What is the agenda going to be for the program?

19. What is the ratio of motivational/inspirational stories versus content or how-to material? (For example, if they are looking for 90% motivational stories, you may not be the best fit for this audience if you are 90% how-to content.)

20. What else if anything can I do to make this program more successful for you?

You do not have to ask every single question on the list. However, consider each that is appropriate for your situation.

Secrets for Before, During, and After Your Speech

Before

1. Send a pre-program survey to attendees to get to know your audience better and also as a sales tool. You can learn a lot about your audience members that may help you later. You could set up individual appointments following your presentation. However, make sure you add value, during your speech, by discussing true solutions to their problems rather than just selling.

2. Get in the Mood – Imagine a time in your past when you felt absolutely fabulous about an accomplishment. See if you can recreate the feeling and hold onto that as you continue to meet your audience and give your speech.

3. How to Stay Calm and Feel Confident – Go to the restroom, find a quiet place, take a deep breath in and tense every muscle in your body for 5 seconds. Then breathe out and release. Do this several times until your body begins to relax. Then, you can stand in a Power Pose,

like Superman – hands on your hips, shoulders back, chin-up, and legs shoulder-width apart. Dr. Amy Cuddy of Harvard University has done all kinds of research about how this Power Pose will help you feel confident within two minutes. If you are still nervous, try panting like a dog for 30 seconds.

4. Greet everyone as if you are the host of your party. Stand at the entrance. Give your audience members a warm handshake. Introduce yourself and begin a brief, warm conversation. Here are the three questions you should ask:

1. What brought you to this event?
2. What were you hoping to get out of this event?
3. Is there anything you were hoping I would cover in my speech?

5. Find out something about someone in the audience to which you can refer, using that person's name, in your speech. This is very important: ask their permission to mention them in your speech.

6. Be sure to put your contact information on every page of your handout so if anyone separates the pages they can still find you.

During

1. Encourage the audience to use social media about your presentation during and after the event. You may even want to say something having already introduced this to your audience, such as "This might be a great time to post about _____."

2. Use audience member names in your speech and insert comments made prior to your speech by them and thank them for that nugget.

3. During your speech, say, "If you would like to have a free article on this topic, write "Article" on the back of your card and hand it to me at the end of my speech. I will make sure you get the "Article." Or, if you prefer, instead of a "Article" you might choose to give an assessment or an ebook instead.

4. Ask questions to engage and get agreement.

5. At the end of your speech, encourage audience members to come and speak with you after your speech.

6. Customize to the audience. Use examples that are relevant to the audience you are speaking to. If they are realtors, use a real estate example. If they sell furniture, use a furniture example.

7. Offer consultations to the group for a reduced fee or special promotion while you're still there.

After

1. Collect evaluation forms and send copies of the positive reviews to the client, saying something like "Here's what people said…" The purpose of an Evaluation Form is two-fold. One is to get favorable quotes you can use and two is to get referrals to other places to speak.

2. Go back to the product table after your session to sign autographs and to answer questions.

3. Create a business card with your contact information on one side and 3 to 5 main points that you

want audience members to remember on the other side. Give them out at your talks. Encourage the attendees to go over these points several times a week. Some people laminate these and pass them out at events.

4. Post your successful talk experience on Facebook and other social media.

5. Follow-up by phone or email with interested parties after the event.

6. Request a testimonial from the meeting planner or program chair.

Evaluation Form
5 Secrets to Being a Great Leader
Evaluation & Questionnaire

NAME _____ COMPANY _____

E-MAIL _____ PHONE/CELL _____ / _____

May we keep in touch with you? ___Yes___No

PLEASE ANSWER THE QUESTONS OR CIRCLE THE OTHERS ON A SCALE FROM 1-10

Do you think the information you received today will be of value to you in your work?   ____Yes   No____

Would you recommend this seminar to others?   ____Yes   ____No

The one thing I learned or liked best from today's seminar was

_____

_____

I received most of the information I expected to receive today:

0   1   2   3   4   5   6   7   8   9   10

Not very much   A lot

I feel committed to using this information to develop my leadership skills

0   1   2   3   4   5   6   7   8   9   10

Not very much   Totally Committed

I would like to meet with Linda to explore going from where I am to where I would like to be. (Circle one)   Yes   No

My speaking business is based on referrals. Who do you know who might enjoy a speech similar to the one you saw today?

Name	Organization	Email	Phone

1.

2.

3.

We promise not to overload your email inbox. We will however, keep in touch with relevant information in regards to solutions for business or career development and to make you aware of special coaching programs or events.

Circle if you would like [Your Name] to send you: [Article Marking Piece] Yes   No

May we quote you? Yes   No

Conclusion:

You deserve to be powerful and successful beyond your wildest imagination. That may sound like an overwhelming challenge, but we know if you stay on track and find the strength inside, you can reach the heights you want to reach. Remember the Magic Mirror in Chapter One. You should be able to look into it now and see so much more than you did before. Now you know how to be more powerful in your leadership, sales, and speaking. Take the time to do the exercises that you've seen in the book and take the steps you need to take to become more powerful.

After all, you have a way to find your North Star and a Magic Formula to achieve anything you can dream. Remember to have fun along the way and enjoy the journey.

You now have the insider secrets to lead others, sell more effectively, and speak with expertise and confidence.

Now you have your marching orders:

Be powerful ... go out and change the world for the better!

CPSIA information can be obtained
at www.ICGtesting.com
Printed in the USA
LVHW07s1200221018
594371LV00011B/264/P

9 781506 905310